HOW TO MAKE $1,000+ A MONTH ONLINE AS A PART-TIME BOOK SCOUT

HOW TO MAKE $1,000+ A MONTH ONLINE AS A PART-TIME BOOK SCOUT

Your Authoritative Guide to Earning a
RISK FREE Income Selling Books,
DVD & CDs to Online Vendors

Perfect for Moms and Dads, Students, Friends of the Library, Fund Raising Organizations—Schools, Churches, Boys and Girls Clubs and Countless other Groups and Individuals

It's Fun, It's Easy, and It's Profitable!

M. MITCH FREELAND
LAS VEGAS BOOK COMPANY
Las Vegas, Nevada

Copyright © 2018 by M. Mitch Freeland
All Right Reserved

Published by Las Vegas Book Company
Las Vegas, Nevada U.S.A

Printed in the United States of America Except as permitted under the United States Copyright Act of 1976, no part of this publication may be reproduced or distributed in any form or by any means, or stored in a database or retrieval system, without the prior written consent of the publisher, except for brief quotations in articles and reviews.

Disclaimer: The publisher and author have used their best efforts in preparing this book; yet they make no representations or warranties to the accuracy or completeness of its contents. Furthermore, the publisher and author disclaim any implied warranties or merchantability or fitness for a particular purpose. The advice and strategies contained in this book may not be suitable for your situation. This book is sold with the understanding that the publisher and author are not engaged in rendering legal, accounting, or other professional services. You should consult with a professional. Neither the publisher nor author shall be liable for any loss of profit or any other commercial damages, including but not limited to special, incidental, consequential, or other damages.

SPECIAL SALES

Books published by Las Vegas Book Company are available at special quantity discounts worldwide to be used for training or for use in corporate promotional programs. Quantity discounts are available to corporations, educational institutions and charitable organizations. Personalized front or back covers can be produced in large numbers.

For information, contact:
www.MitchFreeland.com / MMitchFreeland@gmail.com

1. Home Based Business 2. Personal Development 3. Ecommerce 4. Title: *How to Make $1,000+ a Month Online As a Part-Time Book Scout,*

ISBN: 978-1-7181-6855-8

First Paperback Edition: September 19, 2018

ABOUT THE AUTHOR

Hello, I'm Mitch Freeland. I am the author of *How to Make $1,000+ a Month Online As a Part-Time Book Scout,* published by Las Vegas Book Company. I have bought, sold, scouted, and donated over 500,000 books in the last five years. I have been called "a modern-day polymath" because of the diversity of subjects that appeal to me and for the subjects I write about. I am a person of faith, a business person, and a writer. I write both fiction and nonfiction.

I studied Anthropology at UCLA and started writing at forty-four. Since then, I have written sixty books. Everything I write about, I have experienced. On the fiction side, I have produced six short story collections and a few novels: thrillers, suspense and mystery.

I have been an investor in many young companies and start-ups dealing in all classes of investments for over twenty-five years. I have also been a real estate investor for many years. I have been President and founder of an online bookstore and publishing company (Las Vegas Book Company), Managing Director of private Investment Banking companies, and a hands-on operator in my real estate investing and property management companies. With my brother John, we have bought and sold, fixed and flipped hundreds of single-family and multi-family properties and I have managed over 100 units as a landlord.

Regarding my nonfiction writing, my goal is to create intuitive, pertinent content that can be incorporated into your personal and work life to help you succeed faster and with less stress.

I have started a blog at www.MitchFreeland.com that focuses on strategies for motivation and personal transformation, casino gaming, poker, online bookselling, real estate investing, Christianity and the Bible.

Selected Books by
M. MITCH FREELAND

Bookselling Books

How I Make $4,000 A Month Part-Time Selling Used Books Online

Mastering the Art of Sourcing for Online Booksellers & Collectors

How to Succeed as a Book Scout

Caring for Books (Fall 2018)

How to Identify First Editions (Fall 2018)

Casino Gaming Books

Winning Craps: How to Play and Win Like a Pro. Learn How I Beat the Craps Out of the Casinos for 30 Years

Tested Gambling Systems That Can Make You $100,000+ a Year: Craps, Horses, Poker, Blackjack

How to Play Craps and Win: The 3 Irrefutable Winning Plays and How to Profit from Them

How to Win at Casino Craps

Craps: Basic Strategy for Smart Players

How to Play Baccarat

How to Count Cards at Blackjack

How to Play Blackjack for Beginners and Win! Learn Basic and Advanced Strategies for Optimum Winning Play

Poker Books

The Small Stakes Poker Hustle: How I Make $3,500+ A Month Part-Time Playing $1-2 & $1-3 No-Limit Hold'em & How You Can Too!

Poker Tells and Body Language: How to Substantially Improve Your Income by Studying Your Opponents Mannerisms and Eccentricities

Cash Poker: How to Make $250,000 Over the Next 5 Years Playing Small Stakes Poker (Winter 2018)

The Poker System: How to Play No-Limit Texas Hold'em: A Primer for Smart New Players Who Want to Start with A Winning Edge in the World's Greatest Poker Game

Tactical Player Isolation at No-Limit Hold'em

CONTENTS

INTRODUCTION — 11
Why I am Uniquely Qualified to Write this Book — 12
What is the Aim of This Book? — 12
What Should You Expect in This Book? — 12
Motivator — 14
This Book Scouting Program is Perfect For — 16
In a Nutshell — 17

Chapter 1
GETTING STARTED ON A SOLID FOOTING — 19
Step One: Decide exactly what you want — 19
Step Two: Write down your goals — 20
Step Three: Be willing to pay the price — 20
Step Four: Make a detailed plan — 20
How Important are Plans? — 21
Step Five: Take action on your plan — 24
Step Six: Do something everyday — 24
Step Seven: Never give up — 25

Chapter 2
HOW DOES IT ALL WORK — 27
Where Do You Find the Sales Rank? — 30

Chapter 3
WHERE DO YOU GO FOR BOOKS, DVDs & CDs? — 35
Library Book Sales — 35
Library Book Stores — 36
Retirement Communities / 55 and Older
  Libraries and Bookstores — 37

Estate Sales — 37
Garage Sales — 38
Swap meets & Flea Markets — 38
Thrift Stores — 38
Friends, Relatives and Neighbors — 39
Free Newspapers — 39
Business Cards — 39
Bulletin Boards — 40
Craigslist.org — 40
Church Rummage and Book sales — 41
Religious Books — 45
Leather Bibles — 45
Study Bibles in Particular — 45
Locating Church Book Sales — 46
Colleges and Universities — 46
More about Textbooks — 46
Books NOT to Collect — 47
Most Books Accepted — 48
Most Leather Bound Books and Sets from Fine Reprint Publishers — 48

Chapter 4
WHERE TO SELL YOUR BOOKS, DVDs, CDs AND VIDEO GAMES — 51

Popular Websites that Buy Books — 52
Bookscouter.com — 54
Bonavendi.com — 55
Smartphone Apps — 56
Don't Ship Junk — 60
DVDs and CDs — 60
Recent Transactions — 61

Don't Ship Incomplete Items — 62
Multiple Copies of the Same Item — 63
New Items — 65
Equipment — 65
Packing Materials and Shipping — 65

Chapter 5
QUESTIONS ON BUYBACKS — 67
PayPal® FAQ — 70

Chapter 6
YOUR STEP-BY-STEP ACTION PLAN: A FIVE STEP PROGRAM GETTING STARTED — 73
Length of Time Which you Should Hold a Product — 74
Step 1: Getting your Equipment in Order:
The Things You'll Need — 74
Step 2: Sign up with Bookscouter.com and Bonavendi.com — 76
Step 3: Begin Scanning Items — 76
Step 4: Packing and Shipping Sold Items — 77
Step 5: Grow Your Profits through Sourcing — 77

APPENDIX 1
Frequently Asked Questions For Book Scouting at Library Book Sales — 79

Would You Like to Know More? — 86
What's Next? — 87
Get Your FREE Book — 93
More Books by M. Mitch Freeland— 94
SPECIAL SALES — 96
Book Scouting Log— 97
Preferred BuyBack Websites— 100
Preferred Scouting Venue— 101

INTRODUCTION

"Being a profitable online book scout is easier than most people might think. With a little knowledge you'll make money the first hour you begin."

Starting out as a book scout may be the perfect money generating idea for you. If you like books, movies and music, like being around them, and you like to treasure hunt, then you may have just found the ideal home-based business.

First of all, before we begin, I want to be crystal clear that this book is for new book scouts; however, it is *not* a simple introduction to locating (scouting) valuable books and other media products. The material that I have assembled in this book will allow you to make money full or part-time. I give you everything you will need to start and move you forward in this enterprise. Being a profitable book scout is not difficult or complicated. In fact, the process is rather easy to emulate and anybody who puts in the effort can be a success.

You may be asking: What is a book scout in the first place? First off, a book scout is not a book dealer or somebody who sells books to the public. A book scout is someone who finds used books of value and then sells them to online book dealers and to brick and mortar bookstores. Scouts do this usually with a mobile phone connected to the internet when they get pricing information from a dealer (websites), who purchase books and other media products. Scouts can also use a look-up tool with a service that gives them current prices of books, DVDs, and CDs. The look-up tool is typically a mobile phone or PDA with a scanner that scans barcodes that gives you the going price of the item currently offered online. There are even free Apps available for your mobile phone that allows you to get the information you need wherever you are. This gives you the ability to buy an item to resell from almost anywhere.

There are over forty companies that buy books, DVDs, and CDs online. This book will focus primarily on selling your items to online vendors.

Why I am Uniquely Qualified to Write this Book

I have sold over 200,000 books online and thousands of dollars worth of books, DVDs and CDs to online booksellers and other vendors. I sold used books on Amazon, eBay, Barnes & Noble, Alibris, Abebooks and dozens of other bookselling websites nationally and internationally. I have also sold countless books, DVDs and CDs to online vendors as a scout.

As an online seller for many years, I learned that not everything sells quickly. I learned how to make money selling unsellable items to other online vendors who are willing to pay cash for slow turnover items. I also learned that there is a market for almost everything somewhere.

I have been an Amazon Pro seller for over six years and have a 100% Positive customer rating on eBay.

What is the Aim of This Book?

The aim of this book is to teach you how to make money as a book scout quickly and easily. If executed correctly your financial risk is nil to negligible, because proper book scouting has your buyers already set up and you will know in advance of the price they will pay you for your books, DVDs and CDs. Within moments of picking up a book you will know how much, or how little, a dealer or vendor will pay for that book.

What Should You Expect From This Book?

There are four main areas that will be covered in this book that will prep you for success:

1) Planning to be a success—Getting started on a solid footing

2) How Does it All Work

3) Souring activity and where to get books and other media products to sell to vendors

4) Where to sell your items for quick turnover

You will receive a step-by-step plan of action in Chapter 5.

Chapter 1
First off, we are going to set a course for planning your success. In this section (Motivator), you are going to get started on the right footing by setting plans, goals, and objectives. As with any venture you have to know what you want to get where you want to go.

Chapter 2
How Does it All Work. You will be surprised at the ease of getting started and making money online.

Chapter 3
Sourcing refers to "a number of procurement practices aimed at finding, evaluating and engaging suppliers of goods and services." In our practice, our goods are books, DVDs and CDs. In this section you will learn where and how to attain items to sell.

Chapter 4
Chapter 4 is comprised of a list of over 40 online outfits that are willing to offer you prices on books, DVDs, and CDs.

Chapter 5
Covered here are the most frequently asked questions on buybacks.

Chapter 6
Here you will get your step-by-step plan of action. This is your outline for getting started

Motivator

Dear Future Book Scout:

Imagine…

- Escaping from the day-to-day grind and telling your boss, "Goodbye and Good luck!" (this is if you decide to go full-time)
- Living almost anywhere.
- Having a wonderful day at the beach with friends and family knowing you're making money as you play—books, DVDs and CDs are everywhere.
- Getting out of debt and leaving money worries behind.
- Working less, playing more and being free to do the things you like—and best of all, spending more time with your family and the ones you care about.

Once you understand the simple dynamics that lead to successful book scouting you'll be on your way—and you'll be able to escape all the noise out there, all the commotion that keeps most people out of the game. As the renowned psychologist Abraham Maslow said, you'll be the "self-actualized" individual creating a true and honest future for yourself, knowing exactly what you want and how to attain it—a future of ever expanding growth and opportunity.

This program isn't too good to be true. I've done it and you can too. You're going to see that what I'm about to tell you is straightforward, simple to master, and extremely profitable—and it's practically Risk Free.

Could you see yourself....

- buying a book for 50 cents and selling it a minute later for $7.50. This may not sound like much, but what if you did just five of this type of transactions a day. That's an extra $35 profit a day—everyday. That's $1,050 part-time profit a month. At the end of the year that could make for a nice holiday.
- buying a book for $2 and selling it seconds later for $45.
- buying a book for $1 and selling it seconds later for $22
- buying a book for $1 and selling it seconds later for $65
- buying a DVD for $1 and selling it seconds later for $17
- buying a box of CDs (50) for $5 and selling them minutes later for $50
- buying a book for $1 and selling it one minute later for $95

The aforementioned items were purchased knowing exactly the price they would be resold for to online vendors. There was no financial risk. You only buy what you could sell within seconds. It is easy, secure and financially fun.

If the idea of book scouting is getting you excited, I want to show you another way to make money online. Prior to writing this book I wrote *How I Make $4,000 a Month Part-Time Selling Used Books Online*. I started off part-time, and in no time it turned into a full-time enterprise right from my home. The reason I am mentioning this book to you as this time is that, it is an excellent companion to the book you are holding. After becoming a book scout you might want to investigate the opportunities available in becoming an online book and media seller on Amazon, eBay, Half.com, Barnes & Noble and other websites. So, keep that book in mind when you decide to venture into other online money generating avenues.

BOOK SCOUTING IS <u>NEWBIE FRIENDLY</u> AND IT CAN BE FUN FOR THE WHOLE FAMILY AS A PART-TIME ACTIVITY THAT CAN BE EXTREMELY PROFITABLE

Locating Expensive Books is like Found Buried Treasure

- Have you ever dreamed of high profits with low risk? How about no risk?
- How would you feel about operating your own profitable home based business?
- Have you ever asked yourself: "When am I going to finally step-up and do what I know is right for me? No more waiting. The time has come. The time in NOW!

This Book Scouting Program is Perfect For:

- Stay-at-home moms and dads
- College students
- Retired seniors who want or need more cash flow
- Business owners looking for a solid business with huge potential for growth with zero barriers to entry
- Friends of the Library, Public and Private Libraries in search of funding and managing donations

- Church and nonprofit organizations fundraising by book drives
- People who want to work for themselves at home
- People who want to take immediate control of their own future
- Brand new entrepreneurs wanting to build a new, successful online business that generates income 24/7
- People in need of more cash per month
- Internet booksellers who are unsatisfied with their current performance and want to step-up to another level
- Brick and mortar bookstore owners and employees wanting to jump into the world of online book scouting and wholesaling with a surefire plan and a system to bust records
- Everyone who dreams of a lifestyle change and freedom from the burdens of working for someone else.

In a Nutshell

If you are out of work, short of cash or just starting out, a student, stay-at-home mom or dad, retired senior or someone fed-up with the rat-race and ready for change, church, nonprofit organization or library searching for ways to manage donations effectively with higher cash flow—then this could be the perfect business or fundraiser for you—full-time—part-time or in your spare-time.

As always, I wish you the best of luck in all of your personal and professional endeavors.

M. Mitch Freeland
Los Angeles, CA

Chapter 1

GETTING STARTED ON A SOLID FOOTING

"Good thoughts and actions can never produce bad results; bad thoughts and actions can never produce good results."
—James Allen

I have borrowed this section from my book *How I Make $4,000 a Month Part-Time Selling Used Books Online*, for the singular reason that the concepts presented are critically important to your success. Follow them closely and execute them with precision.

To keep you on the straight and narrow, you'll have to set goals. Brain Tracy, in *Change Your Thinking Change Your Life* holds that there is a "seven-step method for goal setting and achievement". I have used this section in my other books because I feel it is vital for you to start out correctly with goals and plans. Now let's go through this step-by-step:

Step One: Decide exactly what you want. Do you want to make $1,000 a month to supplement your income or $10,000 per month working full-time? Do you want to be a lone ranger working from your home or do you want to grow a business with employees and a warehouse full of books? Deciding exactly what you want can sometimes be a hard thing to do; but think about it and write it down. It can be easier when you have specific needs, monitory needs, family needs, health needs and so on.

Step Two: Write down your goals. It is important that you write down goals. When you write them down they now become concrete, solid and clear—they are not a simple thought or wish. People, who write down their goals, are people who are serious. A curious thing happens when you write down your goals; they become engrained in your mind with the Laws of Attraction and Expectation is now working for you. If you have difficulty determining your goals or the things you want or want to accomplish, clearly, don't be discouraged. Sometimes, all of us have problems with clarity. I wrote a book called *Mini Goals Huge Results*. I wrote the book to help me clarify and achieve my own goals in life. When you have a moment, take a look at it. It could help you define your goals and how to achieve them.

Step Three: Be willing to pay the price. To make your goals come true, you'll have to pay the price. Nothing is for free and the time you spend will have to be time well spent. The Law of Cause and Effect is now in order. You must pay the full price, not half price and not the discount price to achieve your goal. Remember this. There is no such thing as "paying your dues." There really are no free lunches in real life. You do what you have to do to get where you want to go. There are no short cuts to success. The time you spend to achieve your goal is relative.

Step Four: Make a detailed plan. Once your goal is written down, make a plan on how you will achieve it. The way you do this is to make a list prioritizing the most important steps first. For instance, your plan can start with by pulling out your calendar and planning a month or two months scheduling program for sales that are already listed on Booksalefinder.com. Booksalefinder.com is a good website for locating book sales in your area. Your plan could also involve collecting enough books, let's say seventy per week as an example, with an average resale price of $6 (deducting all expenses). You can plan to scout three times per week with a goal of acquiring twenty-four books from each outing—or, once a week acquiring seventy-two books at one sale.

Here is an excerpt from an article I wrote concerning plans that I hope can help demonstrate a point.

How Important are Plans?

Plans measure the person. Without a plan you are virtually an animal existing, not a human being filled with creativity, imagination and dreams.

How important are plans? According to John Steinbeck, plans are crucial. While working on his book, *East of Eden*, Steinbeck wrote a letter addressed to his editor. Novelist, John Steinbeck, winner of the Nobel Prize for literature wrote this about the importance of plans:

> I am going to set down Adam's plans for his life. The fact that he isn't going to get even one of them has no emphasis whatever. Plans are real things and not experience. A rich life is rich in plans. If they don't come off, they are still a little bit realized. If they do, they may be disappointing. That's why a trip described becomes better the greater the time between the trip and the telling. I believe too that if you can know a man's plans, you know more about him than you can in any other way. Plans are daydreaming and this is an absolute measure of a man. Thus if I dwell heavily on plans, it is because I am trying to put down the whole man. What a strange life it is. Inspecting it for greatness. There are strange things in people. I guess one of the things that

sets us apart from other animals is our dreams and our plans. (Maxwell, *Put Your Dream To The Test*, 2009/Steinbeck, Journal of a Novel: *The East of Eden Letters*, 2001)

Plans tell you about the person, his or her dreams, aspirations, and what is important. The measure of a persons plan explains the person, who he or she is and what he or she aspires to become. Great plans make a great person. A big plan shows the world a person's ambition. Small plans show the world a person's lack of ambition, lack of true motivation, and low aspirations.

Yes, a person's plan tells you about the person and tells you about yourself. In the book and subsequent movie, *The Treasure of the Sierra Madre*, Howard, the old prospector asks Curtin about what he will do with the money from his gold prospecting once they pull up stakes. Curtin is humbled and explains he would like to buy land and raise fruit trees, peaches. In his youth he picked fruit in the San Joaquin Valley and loved the camaraderie of the workers sitting around the fire at night and singing until morning. The idea or planting seeds and saplings and watching them grow until fruit is harvested from them must be a great feeling of satisfaction, a great feeling of accomplishment he emphasizes. Curtin has a long-range plan, a dream of doing what he really enjoyed early in his life.

Then Curtin asks the old prospector, Howard, what he plans to do with his fortune. Howard wants of buy a general store for his old age and to live financially secure with the money brought from his gold. Then Curtin asks Dobbs the same question. Dobbs tells Curtin and Howard what he plans to do with his treasure: New fancy clothes, going to the best restaurant in town and ordering everything on the bill of fare; then balling out the waiter even when the food is excellent. "What else?" Curtin asks Dobbs, hoping for a plan of substance rather than short-term gratification and shallowness. Dobbs states, "What else is there?" (Dobbs' question refers to women)

As now realized, both Curtin and Howard had a plan of long-term prospects for their fortunes. Curtin wants to own land and grow fruit trees and harvest fruit. Howard wants a general store for retirement. Howard will have to buy real estate and invest in inventory. Both Curtin and Howard will be investing in real estate; a farm for Curtin and a store for Howard. But Dobbs has no long-term plans; he has no plan of investing his fortune. He wants to spend his money on consumable, depreciating stuff. He wants to spend his money and he wants to be a big shot in the world, because he's small in everything else.

The plans people make tell you about who they are and what they believe in. If you want to get to know someone, ask them about their plans. Their plans will tell you almost everything you want to know about them: the way they think, feel about life, feel about people, their confidence and self-doubts, and naturally, what they truly believe in.

Starting today, make your plans. Think about what you want to achieve and how you are going to achieve it. Write it out, and make your plans. All highly successful people write down plans constantly, all the time, everyday. When you want to focus on your dreams, set your plan and then put it into action. Book selling is a methodical business; it is a planning business—and successful booksellers are voracious planners. You can be a voracious planner, too. So, get to it!

###

Step Five: Take action on your plan. Taking action is the only step that will advance you closer to achieving your goal. Don't wait for the perfect day, time or place. As Zig Ziglar says, "Are you going to wait till all the lights are green before you head into town?" You may not be going anywhere for a longtime if you wait the perfect moment—because there is no perfect moment. Do not wait for the weather to change, the holidays to pass or until you think you need to save some money before you set out to take action. Start small if you must—but start. Do not wait another day to begin—start now. Everything will fall in place once you begin and after a few months you'll see for yourself the progress you'll make with consistent action. Remember this: At this time in your life: (1) you may not be getting any richer; (2) you may feel you are not getting any smarter; and (3) you are not feeling any better; but the only thing you are doing is getting older. So start today. Don't wait another second. Even if you decide to do nothing, the days and months and years will still pass—summer to autumn, autumn to winter, winter to spring, spring to summer—all over again. The cycle doesn't end until you end. And it's not how you start, it's how you finish.

Step Six: Do something everyday. Everyday do something that takes you in the direction of achieving your goals. Your motivation is self-induced when you do something everyday to move yourself forward toward the accomplishment of your goal. Of course, when you decide to make book scouting a full-time profession, you'll definitely do something every day, but if you've decided to start off part-time, it is now crucial for you to do something everyday that moves you in the direction of your goals. This could be calling libraries to confirm sale dates or attending a local garage sale on Saturday morning.

Step Seven: Never give up. If you are committed to be a successful book scout then make up your mind to never give in to the stresses of daily living. As in all business ventures there will be certain pressures, time commitments and some mild aggravations. Accept this as part of your learning process. After a while, you'll learn to deal effectively with temporary setbacks and relish in phenomenal sales and independence. But in the meantime, think through your troubles and then take action. It is always a great idea to write the situation down and then write down ways to make the situation better. Make a list of ten solutions. Sit and think. Your answer will be revealed on your piece of paper.

> *People with goals succeed because they know where they're going.*
> **— Earl Nightingale**

Start setting your goals now. Write them down quickly and then think about them. After you've digested the rest of this book, read your goals frequently and follow the other six steps you'll take to accomplish them; and rewrite them if necessary. Remember: your goals will change all the time. The more competent you before in book acquisition and higher your income grows, you'll set new goals. This is a natural process when you are growing.

When you have a moment, I suggest you get a copy of *Maximum Achievement* by Brian Tracy. To learn more about goals and how to achieve them try *Mini Goals Huge Result*. The book is FREE at my website: www.MitchFreeland.com.

Chapter 2

HOW DOES IT ALL WORK

"Whatever you think, be sure it is what you think; whatever you want, be sure it is what you want; whatever you feel, be sure it is what you feel.
—T. S. Eliot

How does this all work? The ease will surprise you. The scout enters the ISBN number of the book into the bookseller's internet-based system (these are Apps or websites such as Bookscouter.com or individual online vendor websites that buy books, DVDs and CDs).

The ISBN number can be located on many places on the book: back cover, copyright page, lower rear dust jacket cover or upper front flap. The ISBN can be the 10 digit or 13 digit numbers, and commonly starts with 978. A price will pop up showing the scout how much the bookseller is willing to pay for the book or a statement will show that the book is not currently being purchased by that particular vendor. Different websites offer different amounts depending on many factors, but the biggest factor is demand for the item which can be characterized with a low Amazon sales rank. The lower the sales rank, the higher the current demand is for the item A book with a sales rank of 1,000 will generally sell within 24 hours (if priced competitively), whereas a book with a sales rank of 100,000 may take 30 days to sell. A rank of 1,000,000 may take several months to a year to sell, and items with an Amazon sales rank of 5 million could take a year or much longer if you were to open an Amazon seller's account and post the book for sale. The lower the sales rank, the more a book dealer is willing to pay because the turnover is quick. There is demand for the book.

Here is an approximate rundown of Amazon sales rank and the number of books that sell under the ranking:

Amazon Sales Rank	# of Books Sold in 24 hour period
1 – 10	700 – 3,000
10 – 100	500 – 700
100 – 500	200 – 500
500 – 1000	140 – 200
1,000 – 2,000	70
2,000 – 3,000	49
3,000 – 4,000	40
4,000 – 5,000	24
5,000 – 6,000	21
6,000 – 7,000	18
7,000 – 8,000	15
8,000 – 9,000	12
9,000 – 10,000	12
10,000 – 11,000	11
11,000 – 12,000	10

12,000 – 13,000	10
13,000 – 14,000	9
14,000 – 15,000	8
15,000 – 16,000	7
16,000 – 17,000	6
17,000 – 18,000	6
18,000 – 19,000	7
19,000 – 20,000	5
20,000 – 21,000	6
21,000 – 22,000	5
22,000 – 23,000	5
23,000 – 24,000	6
24,000 – 25,000	5
25,000 – 26,000	5
26,000 – 27,000	5
29,000 – 30,000	4
30,000 – 31,000	4
31,000 – 32,000	4
32,000 – 33,000	4
33,000 – 34,000	2
34,000 – 35,000	2
35,000 – 36,000	2
36,000 – 37,000	2
37,000 – 38,000	2
38,000 – 39,000	2
39,000 – 40,000	2
40,000 – 41,000	2
41,000 – 42,000	2
42,000 – 50,000	1.5
50,000 – 60,000	1.5
60,000 – 70,000	1.3
70,000 – 80,000	0.8
80,000 – 90,000	0.7
90,000 – 100,000	0.6

100,000 – 110,000	0.4
110,000 – 120,000	0.5
140,000 – 150,000	0.2
150,000 – 160,000	0.1
160,000 – 170,000	0.1
170,000 – 500,000	0

Where Do You Find the Sales Rank?

When you scroll down on the Amazon sales page of your item, the sales rank will be on the left side of the page under the title *Product Details*. It will say *Amazon Best Sellers Rank*

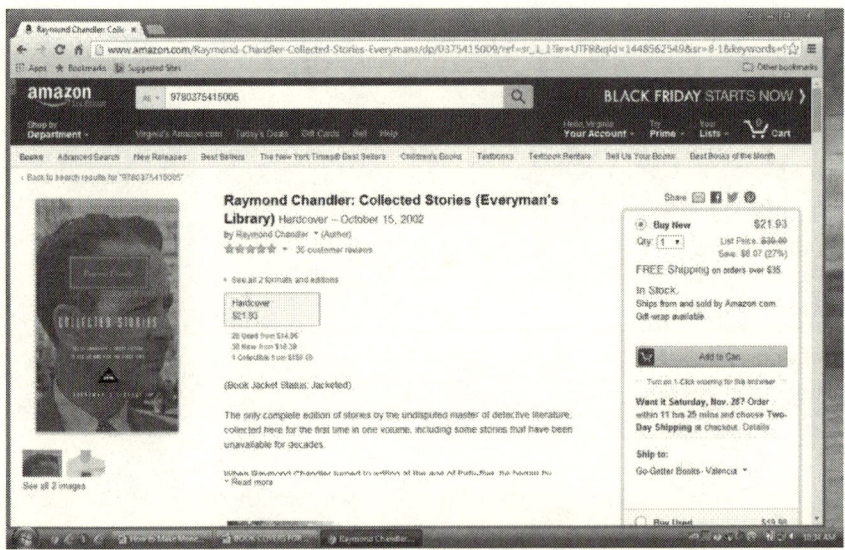

Scroll down on the sales page.

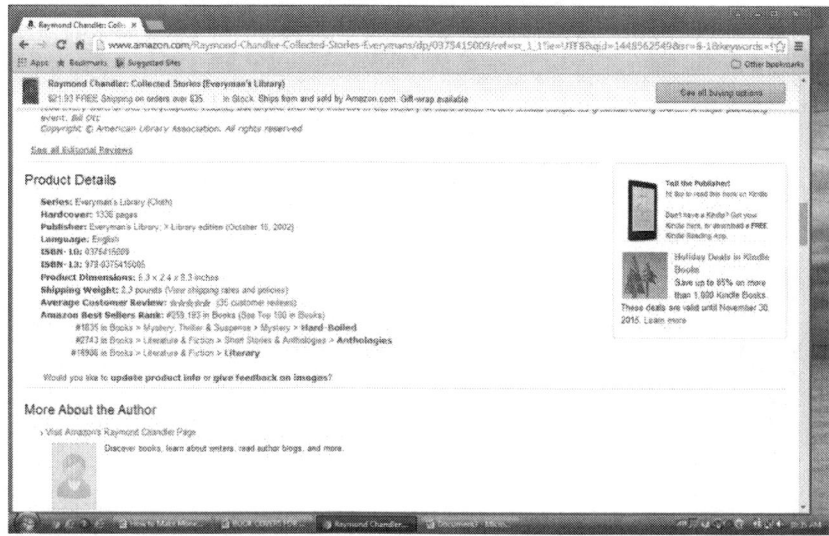

I have highlighted the Amazon Best Sellers Rank below.

Product Details

- **Series:** Everyman's Library (Cloth)
- **Hardcover:** 1336 pages
- **Publisher:** Everyman's Library; X-Library edition (October 15, 2002)
- **Language:** English
- **ISBN-10:** 0375415009
- **ISBN-13:** 978-0375415005
- **Product Dimensions:** 5.3 x 2.4 x 8.3 inches
- **Shipping Weight:** 2.3 pounds (View shipping rates and policies)
- **Average Customer Review:** 4.8 out of 5 stars See all reviews (35 customer reviews)
- **Amazon Best Sellers Rank:** #259,193 in Books (See Top 100 in Books)

Here is another screenshot: The Amazon Best Sellers Rank is highlighted below.

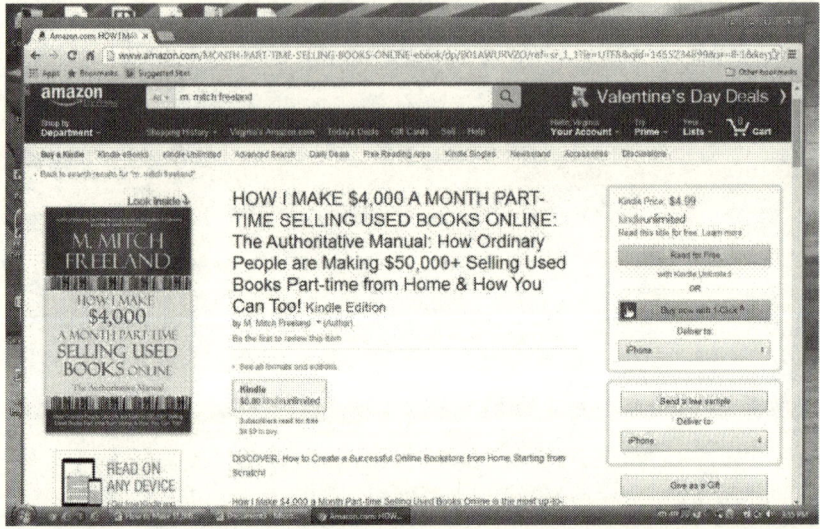

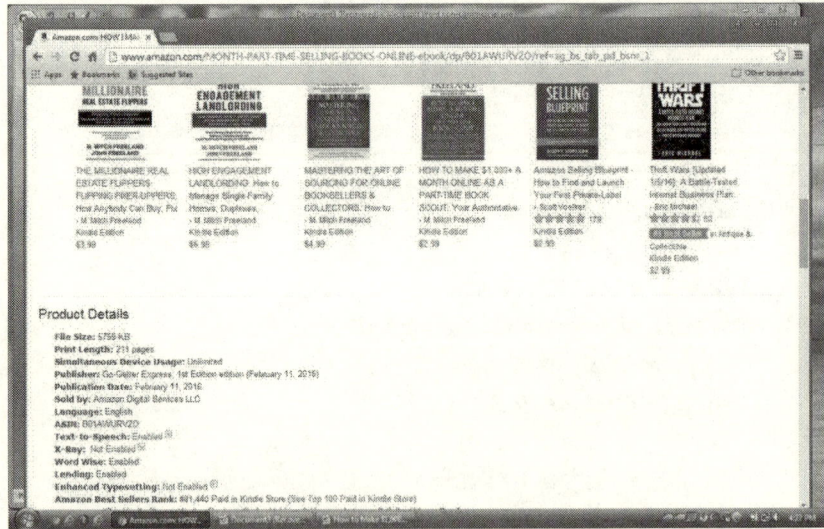

On this screenshot the Amazon Sales Rank is at the very bottom.

32

Product Details

- **File Size:** 5759 KB
- **Print Length:** 211 pages
- **Simultaneous Device Usage:** Unlimited
- **Publisher:** Go-Getter Express; 1st Edition (February 11, 2016)
- **Publication Date:** February 11, 2016
- **Sold by:** Amazon Digital Services LLC
- **Language:** English
- **ASIN:** B01AWURVZO
- **Enhanced Typesetting:** Not Enabled
- **Amazon Best Sellers Rank:** #81,440 Paid in Kindle Store (See Top 100 Paid in Kindle Store)

The lower the Amazon sales rank the more an online dealer is willing to pay for the book. But only when the demand is high and supply short, is when prices rise. If there are hundreds of books available, the price may stay low until the heavy supply is absorbed. This is particularly important with expensive textbooks. For example: I attended my local library book sale, which is held once a month. I located three textbooks: Advanced Calculus, Chemistry and American History.

The Advanced Calculus book scanned at $80. It had a sales rank of 2,500, which indicated that the book was currently very popular and on Amazon was selling approximately 49 copies a day or that particular day. Many book dealers had a buyback set at 50% of the Amazon low price of $80. So, when I went to a couple of the buyback websites they offered me $40 for the book. I paid $3 for the book at the library book sale. My profit would be $37 on this one book.

The Chemistry book was ranked 90,000, and the low price on Amazon was $25 to buy. A buyback site offered $6.25, or 25% of the low Amazon retail price. My cost was $3, so I would still make a $3.25 profit.

Lastly, the American History book scanned at $55 with a sales rank of 35,000, and a buyback site offered to buy it for $18.50. My cost again was $3. I would make a profit of $15.50 on this one book.

My profit for the three books was $55.50. The price of the buyback is determined by the current price and popularity of the book in question. The more popular, the higher the price a dealer is willing to pay. This is because the dealer is betting on a fast turnover. Once the book is received by the dealer, it is listed, and with a low sales rank, and some luck, it will be sold in a few days. Higher ranked books could take several months to sell and dealers are leery to hold books for long periods of time in which they have a high capital investment. As with all solid businesses, cash flow is king—turnover of inventory must be in a reasonable time frame, taken into account of the price paid for the inventory.

At check-out a FREE postage label is printed and the scout ships the book(s) to the dealer. Most scouts will ship numerous books in a box. A Paypal payment is almost immediate when the dealer receives the books and processes your order. Check payment is also available for scout's convenience. I prefer PayPal. It is much faster and less hassle. If you do not have a PayPal account I suggest opening one up. You will get payment a lot faster than having to wait for a check in the mail. Recently, I mistakenly pressed the *check* instead of PayPal for payment and the check took nearly two weeks longer than had I used PayPal. You can, with a couple of clicks, move your PayPal funds to your bank account. The transfer is free and you will receive it in usually two to four days.

Chapter 3

WHERE DO YOU GO FOR BOOKS, DVDs & CDs?

"Sources for Books, DVDs and CDs are practically everywhere: Libraries, neighbors, swap meets, garage sales, etc...."

In this section you are going to be introduced to several of the more popular sources for finding resalable books, DVDs and CDs. If your plan is make over $1,000 per month, then you will need to spend the time and energy to search for products to sell. Don't underestimate the time it will take you to scout for products. If you are in a city with many sources, great; however, if you are in a rural area, you will need to venture out and be more creative in your scouting activities. During any given month I will travel, on average, over fifty miles to a library sale. And usually, I will travel over one hundred miles each way to collect a sizable booty of 50 to 200 books that are sellable online to vendors.

Library Book Sales

Your local library is one of your first choices for books. Check with public and private libraries in your area regarding their book sales. Libraries will have sales headed by "The Friends of the Library" organization. Sales are typically scheduled monthly, quarterly, semi-annually or annually—it all depends on the size of the library and the number of books and other media donations they receive. Make it a plan to call or search online for all libraries in your vicinity. I typically travel fifty miles or more to attend good library book sales since most items are sold for $2 and under.

A good library sale will harvest upwards of fifty or more quality books sellable from $2 up. The nice thing about a library sale is that, you will have your books in under an hour when the doors open.

Some "Friends of the Library" organizations have a preview sale for members. This preview is well worth the annual membership which is anywhere from $5 to $45 annually. The preview sale is for members only and is held before the general public sale. The sale is usually in the morning before the general sale or evening before the general sale.

Library book sales are competitive. You will need to be quick and dedicated to get your share. Get to the sale early, before the doors open. In fact, lines start forming an hour or more before the doors open. So, you want to be one of the first ones in. After a few outings, you will get a quick education of what you will have to do to get your share of the quality books. Know where the textbooks and nonfiction books are located and get there first. The more sales you attend the better you will become scouting. Speed has a lot to do with your success, but if you are able to get into the room before the hoards and inspect the books prior to the sale—even better. Talk to the organizers of the sale about getting in earlier. Many organizations will let you buy a few books before the sale starts if you volunteer to help set up. This could take an hour or more of your time, but the rewards could be significant.

Library Book Stores

Many libraries have small bookstores in the library. Check the library bookstores regularly. Donations are brought in daily, so make it a habit to drop in every chance you get. Most bookstores do not have an attendant. The store is usually a little room or a few shelves full of books.

The honor system is in play here. Most times you will pay for your books at the customer service desk or leave money in a drop-box. In most library book stores you will find both fiction and nonfiction books, and a few DVDs and CDs. Unlike a library book sale, the library book store is typically not busy, so here you could take time without feeling rushed.

Retirement Communities / 55 and Older Libraries and Bookstores

Many retirement communities have their own libraries and used bookstores. The prices for books are usually $0.50 for paperbacks and $1-$2 for hardcovers. If you live in one of these communities you should definitely visit the bookstore at least once per week. If you have family or friends who can get you into the facility, then by all means go. I have found the bookstores to be a solid goldmine with virtually no competition. In fact, if you are retired, living in the community, and visit the bookstore four times per month, you could make a few hundred dollars without having to scout anywhere else.

Estate Sales

Estate sales can be a good source for books especially when the estate of a collector or avid reader or educator is up for sale. Estate sale prices are typically reasonable and similar to library book sales prices. The best way to locate sales is on Craigslist.org or doing a search online in your area. On Craigslist.org, type in your city or area, then type in "Estate Sale." Estate sales are usually held early morning on Fridays and Saturdays and you should plan to get there early since lines begin to form an hour before the doors open.

When you search for sales in your area, be certain to also check that there will be lots of books for sale. Also, when you have a phone number of the Estate Sales organizer or agent, ask about books, DVDs and CDs. One estate sale I attended had limited books but was a goldmine of brand new CDs and many DVDs. The former owner of the items was a collector and I ended up purchasing over two hundred items in about ninety minutes. I paid $200 for the lot. The resalable value of the lot was over $5,000 on Amazon, and the buyback prices were over $800. I had a nice profit selling them on Amazon and the rest I sold to other dealers online to clear out my inventory.

Garage Sales

Garage or yard sales can be good places to search for salable items. Again, the easy way is to check on Craigslist.org for garage sales in your area. Sales that say books, DVDs, lots of CDs are the sales you want to go to. After you have pin pointed the sales you what to attend, make a plan to get there early—at daybreak—six to seven in the morning.

Swap meets & Flea Markets

Usually, Saturdays and Sundays are Swap meet days. Here you will always find books, DVDs and CDs. Swap meets differ in size. Search the internet for swap meets in your area; they are good places to meet regular sellers and collectors. Keep names and numbers and always ask questions. Always ask vendors if they have more books or DVDs at home that they want to sell. This question has gotten me tenfold as many items than what I would generally pick up at a Saturday or Sunday swap meet. Now you can meet sellers at their homes, in a leisure setting and go through there items, picking out the things you want.

Thrift Stores

Some thrift stores are better than other. A lot depends on the price charged for books, DVDs and CDs. In some communities thrift stores like Goodwill and Salvation Army charge $1.99 for softcovers and $2.99 up for hardcovers. Others charge $.99 for softcovers and $1.49 for hardcovers. As you can see, the price you pay can determine whether you leave with five books or fifteen books. Other, mom and pop stores could have reasonable prices or prices completely out of whack. Thrift stores in your area are worth a try. Some will pay off well and other may not be worth your while. You will have to visit them regularly before you make an informed decision to stick with it.

Friends, Relatives and Neighbors

Everybody has stuff they want to get rid of. Ask friends and relative if they have books and other media products they do not want. Spring cleaning is a good time to ask neighbors before they have their garage sales. Most times you won't even have to pay for the items.

Free Newspapers

Most communities have a free newspaper. You can peruse through the paper quickly once a week looking for books no longer wanted.

Business Cards

When you are in it, get all the way in it. Get business cards printed and let everyone you know that you are looking for books, DVDs and CDs— and don't forget video games.

> # I BUY
> ## BOOKS, DVDs, CDs, Video Games
> ## FOR CASH
>
> ### JIMMY BOOKSCOUT
> ### CALL NOW: 555-555-5555
> DONATIONS ACCEPTED • PICK UP AVAILABLE

Leave your business cards everywhere you go.

Bulletin Boards

Posting your cards or a flyer on local bulletin boards is a free idea. Supermarkets, school bulletin boards and senior housing developments are a good start. Whenever you see a bulletin board, attach your info to it—a card or flyer.

Craigslist.org

Searching Craigslist is easy. Posting "I buy books" is easy to. Do this regularly and you will continually receive calls or emails of people who have what you want. You could also post "I will pick up your books for free." Or "Donate your books—FREE pick up." You might end up with a lot of junk that is not sellable, but on occasion you will get a collection of winners that make it worth the while.

Church Rummage and Book sales

I like church book sales. The competition is light and prices are right. Many churches and synagogues hold annual or semi-annual book sales for fund raising. These sales are typically very good, and most host a variety of books. Many of these sales are similar in size of monthly library book sales, offering three thousand to five thousand books—some even offer over ten thousand books along with CDs, DVDs. The great thing about these sales is that most booksellers and resellers miss them, especially when they are not heavily advertised on known book sales websites.

Look for church sales on craigslist.org and pay particular attention to local advertisements. Since many are poorly advertised, it is good for you and you have an excellent chance of collecting a significant haul of valuable books. Sales are usually held on Saturdays and Sundays, after services. Sometimes they are held on weekdays, particularly Friday.

Most church sales do not advertise on **Booksalefinder.com** or other websites, so you've got to be diligent. Check on craigslist or call the religions establishments in your area and simply ask if they are having a book sale or rummage sale anytime soon—and if they give you a date, set it on your calendar and plan to arrive early—right when they open the sale. One strategy you want to take is to see the books before the sale. When you call, explain that you are a book scout and you'll be buying a lot of books and if you can purchase books before the sale. You want to state that you'd gladly pay more than their sales day prices. You can even offer a price a bit higher than what they planned to sell them for to the public.

Here is a program you could offer to Church sales organizers. This is a program I offered to Friends of the Library organizations:

Book Purchase Program

The vast benefits the Friends of the Library and your Library receive when enrolled in the Go-Getter Book Purchase Program include:

Immediate Payment without risk. We are the only organization that we know of that will write you a check the same day the inventory leaves your possession. Therefore, there is no risk of losing inventory. Other organizations have you do all the work and send the inventory to them. Then they list the books online to sell. When your books sell they keep a large percentage and promise to send you the balance. From experience we know it can take months to sell a book on the internet. Who wants to do all that work then wait for a check? Here, you are at risk. Under our program there is no risk.

Minimal Volunteer Hours Needed. You do very little work under our program. All we ask is that you show us your inventory, give us a few hours to go through the inventory and then we write you a large check. We do the sorting, stacking, boxing and shipping ourselves. Under the other programs your volunteers do the sorting, stacking, scanning, cleaning, boxing and shipping of the books. Wow! Who wants to do all that work and still have inventory leave your premises without getting paid.

No Shipping Required. Although we believe these other companies to be reputable, why would anyone risk shipping large amounts of inventory with the hope to get paid sometime in the future? Businesses fail all the time. Mail is lost all the time. Unscrupulous employees steal all the time. There is no need to take this risk. With us there is NO Risk Now, NO Risk Later, and No Risk Ever.

No Risk Ever. We pay you one large check the day the inventory leaves your premises. The other organizations piecemeal you a check every time they sell a book on the internet. Under the other organizations model the organization has no risk. They do not buy your inventory; they sell your inventory over the internet. Here, you have all the risk. Under our program you have No Risk—we take all the risk.

Speed of Funding. We can act very quickly and purchase your inventory within 72 hours (sometimes sooner) at first contact, and have a check in your hand. This can be very beneficial if you are having cash flow issues and simply can't wait for your next public sale.

No Contracts. We do not require you to sign any contracts. Other organizations have you sign one year contracts. We understand that a contract is only good as long as everyone is happy. However, if you would feel more comfortable with a contract we will accommodate you.

We Donate Books to You. Occasionally, we receive large donations that don't fit our purchase and sales criteria. These donations are recycled by donating back to you to be sold at your public sale.

We Pay You 130%. We will purchase on average 10% of your inventory at a premium of 130% of your normal public sale prices. For Example: if you typically sell 10% of your inventory for $1,000 we will write you a check for $1,300. It's that simple. That is 30% more –directly to your bottom line. If you charge $0.50 for paperbacks, we will buy them for $.065. If you charge a $1.00 for hardcover books, we will buy them for $1.30.

No Costs, Fees or Charges. To enroll in our Program there are no costs, fees or charges. We are merely purchasing your inventory on a regular basis.

Less Sorting, Stacking and Cleaning. We save your volunteers many hours of sorting, stacking, cleaning, pricing, boxing and displaying the 10% of the inventory that we purchase.

More than books are purchased. We purchase not only your books but also CDs, DVDs, and Video Games.

Sell More at Public Sales Events. You will sell more books at your public sales, because some of the book dealers will lower their criteria and some of the more aggressive book dealers who make the sales feel competitive will stop attending, therefore making the events more welcoming for public customers. In a more hospitable environment those customers that shied away because of the competitive environment will make their presence once again.

More Money to You. You will have more money with less effort to support your organization and its events.

I particularly like church book sales for the very fact that, when they are poorly advertised, I will be one of only two or three serious buyers. Sometimes I will be the only serious buyer—and when this is the case, I clean up. The strategy for these sales is to arrive early, being the first one is always a good, profitable habit. As I write this section, I've recently attendant two church sales in the past two days—one Saturday morning, prior to a library sale, which started at ten (the church sale began at eight), and one Sunday afternoon. I usually prefer not to work on Sundays, but I logically deducted that the professional crowd would be small or nil on Sunday afternoon (the sale was held after services). I purchased fifty two books from the first sale and forty-seven from the other (approximately two boxes filled from each sale). I had arrived twenty minutes late for the Sunday sale and to my dismay found two other book sellers already with a cart and box full of books. They left shortly after my arrival and as I mentioned, I still collected forty-seven books. Also, make a habit of scanning the floor, tables and shelves three or four times over. And do not neglect to look under tables and in sealed boxes before you decide to cash out. Sometimes new books are added to the tables and frequently you will simply look over books worth taking. At the Sunday sale I found a box that had not been opened, under a table. I opened it and found six good books. Sometimes, volunteers forget to open the boxes or forget to place boxes on tables.

Religious Books

You would think that church and other religious organization book sales would have a high degree of religious books, bibles and religious study material: but to contrary belief, I've found that this is not the case; however, you can find, perhaps, just a little more in this category at a good church sale. I am particularly fond of religious books of all religions, Study Bibles, Hymn books, and most other books relating to spirituality, God, and philosophy. The aforementioned books are not cyclical by nature, as text books are. During the coming New Year, in the months of December and January, sales are slightly higher when people take a new look at theirs or others mortality because of the holiday season and the new year.

Leather Bibles

Most leather Bibles that are within a few years old and in good condition are resalable. Check the copyright page for the correct ISBN. Many Bibles and Study Bibles come in different colors and will have a different ISBN for each color. Naturally, when it is free of notations in the text or underlining or writing on the presentation page, it is more desirable.

Study Bibles in Particular

Study Bibles in good condition sell well and are worth the price of a dollar or two. The better ones are large, hardcover books with dust jackets—other good books are leather bound. Study Bibles are up in my ranks as consistent sellers. But you will always need to scan them first before you make an investment. You need current study bibles by popular (T.V.) personality preachers.

If you come across many new editions of clean leather bibles free on markings try stopping into a local used bookstore to see if they are interested.

Locating Church Book Sales

The easiest way to search for church book sales is on craigslist.org. Simply choose your city and then type in "books church". It's that easy. You can also try "church rummage sale" since the word "rummage" is used frequently. If the word "books" is not used in advertisement, try calling before the sale. Sometimes the individual who posts the ad might have forgotten to list book offerings. If there is a phone number always call and ask about books, DVDs and CDs. And always get there early before the doors open.

Colleges and Universities

Textbooks are the cream of the crop when it comes to finding expensive books. Most students will sell books back at the end of the semester or quarter. Some campus bookstores will not pay much for books in poor condition or when the new edition is coming out soon. When this is the case, some of these books still hold value.

If you are in school you can ask friends and other students for the books that they no longer want. You can also ask professors and instructors. Get lots of business cards made up and start handing them out. Everybody on a college campus has books, and here you will have to work the numbers game. You may be suddenly surprised at what you get.

More about Textbooks

As a scout, textbooks ought to be the number one type of book you should be scouting for. Current textbook prices, on average, offer a much higher buyback percentage paid out. Textbooks can be anything from smaller paperback books used for literature classes or heavy math and science books that run $150 used. In many scenarios, buyback vendors are willing to pay 30% to 50% of the going price of Amazon's retail prices, depending on the demand for the book.

Books NOT to Collect

- No Readers Digest or Time Life books and sets
- No Encyclopedia sets or dictionaries*
- No Pornography
- No International Editions of Textbooks
- No Magazines or Calendars
- No Workbooks with missing pages or heavy writing (books with pages intact and minor writing are all right)
- No books without front covers. Hardcovers should have jackets unless issued without
- No Advance Reading copies, Uncorrected Proofs or Galleys
- No books stating "Not for Resale" or "Review" copy stamps
- No custom edition textbooks designed for one school or international editions
- No foreign books (Spanish books are acceptable)
- No small paper backs (pulp) or Novels (Although modern first editions in "Very Good" condition can be valuable, they are few and far between. Most fiction is not worth it unless you know a great deal about them. Therefore, it's best your helper not waste time with them. Nonfiction is more productive).
- No old travel guides

- No badly damaged books, books with mold or heavy soiling
- No cassette tapes
- No cracked CDs or DVDs or heavily scratched disks

*Encyclopedia sets could be purchased if sets are in "New" condition or no more than two years old. Older published sets are not a good idea to purchase for resale. Not only is shipping more expensive, but many older sets are almost always worthless anymore with easily accessible information online.

Most Books Accepted

- Engineering (less than 5 years old)
- Medical textbooks (less than 5 years old)
- Architecture
- Art and Art Instructional books
- Math and Science (less than 5 years old, preferably less than 3 years old)

Most Leather Bound Books and Sets from Fine Reprint Publishers

- Easton Press (leather) (does not have ISBN)
- Franklin Library (leather) (does not have ISBN)
- Folio Society (non-leather, with slipcase) (does not have ISBN)
- Modern Library (most titles accepted, non- leather) (ISBN—older editions do not have ISBN)
- Everyman's Library (most titles accepted, non-leather) (ISBN—older editions do not have ISBN)
- The Library of America (most titles accepted, non-leather, most with slipcase) (ISBN)

These books do not have ISBN (International Standard Book Number) numbers. The ISBN is the book's identifier. It is the 10 or 13 digit number on the rear barcode or on the publisher's copyright page. Any of these books purchased for $3 and under are excellent buys.

Books without ISBN, such as Easton Press or Folio Society books cannot be priced automatically with online dealers. In this situation you should email the dealer, letting them know what you have and if they are interested. Be descriptive in your email: include, year of publication, slipcase included, and condition of book.

Note: Books published by Folio Society and The Library of America come with slipcases. A slipcase is a big plus, but not necessarily required.

You can also call on your local used bookstore to see how much they are willing to pay for these types of books. If you happen to live in Portland, Oregon, you could stop in at Powell's Bookstore. They buy used books directly from the store and online. I have sold books to Powell's online and simply shipped them in.

Chapter 4

Where to Sell Your Books, DVDs, CDs and Video Games

"The man who is prepared has his battles half fought."
--Miguel deCervantes

There are quite a few places online to sell your books. And some will accept DVDs, CDs, and video games as well. I do not do much business in video games, but there is a market when you find the right products. The list of organizations that buy books online changes constantly. Since reliable software programs dictate the prices that online buyback vendors will pay, the buyback prices of each organization will be different. For instance, the buyback for current textbooks is very competitive and many dealers will buy books for 50 percent of Amazon's retail prices. This means that a book priced on Amazon for $80 (lowest price) could be sold to an online dealer for $40. The dealer would buy your book for $40 and then attempt to sell it on its own website, on Amazon, or on another market place for $80 or more. Naturally, the dealer would have to pay all the Amazon commissions and fees for selling. As a scout you are paid $40 flat, without fees or postage, which is usually free.

Most buyback sites will allow you to print out a postage paid mailing label that you could print out and affix to your package or box. The process is easy. We will go over the complete process step-by-step later in the book.

Popular Websites that Buy Books

1. Buyback101.com
2. **TopDollar4Books.com**
3. **BookItBuyback.com** (has changed to **BuyBackExpress.com**)
4. **CKYBooks.com**
5. Bookstores.com
6. K-12BookBuyer.com
7. RentText.com
8. TextBooksRush.com
9. **TextBookRecycling.com**
10. Cash4Books.net
11. BookJingle.com
12. **Textbooks.com**
13. BlueRocketBooks.com
14. **Bookbyte.com**
15. **SellBackYourBook.com**
16. Chegg.com
17. ValoreBooks.com
18. **PowellsBooks.com**
19. BarnesandNoble.com
20. Booksintocash.com
21. MyBookMonkey.com
22. Recycle-A-Textbook.com
23. CentralCityBooks.com
24. iSellTextbooks.net
25. SellAText.net
26. TextbookManiac.com
27. Abebooks.com
28. Etextshop.com
29. Marathonbooks.com

30. SellBackBooks.com
31. BookMonster.com
32. Dorksbooks.com
33. BooksCashed.com
34. Amazon.com/Book Buyback (Credit No Cash)
35. FreeTextbooks.com
36. BookEmporium.com
37. eCampus.com
38. MyBookCart.com
39. PhatCampus.com
40. TextbookStop.com

The buyback companies I've marked in bold are the ones I've used in the past. The ones with the fasted payments and seem to do more buying are:

- SellBackYourBook.com (they also have a company that buys DVDs and CDs, SellBackYourDVDsandCDs.com (Free Shipping for both)
- BookItBuyBack.com (BuyBackExpress.com)
- TextBookRecycler.com
- Cash4Books.net
- TopDollar4Books.com
- Bookbyte.com (Bookbyte high quotes for a lot of books. They are very competitive on buyback pricing)

A very large percentage of the books that I have sold to buyback websites have had Amazon rankings over 1 million. In fact, I would say that the average ranking was about 4 million. The books were not liquid, meaning, if you had posted the books for sale on your Amazon Sellers Account, it would probably take 12 months, and likely longer to sell the books. Moreover, I had many of the books listed on a number of websites for well over a year and some over two or three years. They were listed competitively, but did not sell. I eventually sold them to online vendors and made a surprisingly good profit.

Bookscouter.com

Go to www.Bookscouter.com. Scan in your books, or type in the ISBN number. The best price will come up with dealers quoting, a price they are willing to pay for your book. Not all buyback sites will want your book. Some companies might have a waiting list of someone who might want your book. If this is the case, they will offer more for the book. For instance, I have an art book with a rank of 3,000,000. The Amazon selling price was $27, and there was only one dealer who posted a price to buy it. The price was $7. No other dealer offered a price. Now this could be a software error on the dealer's side, but most dealers will honor the price quoted when they receive the book.

Bookscouter.com is your first choice for locating the highest price a book will fetch from a buyback vendor. You scan in or type in the ISBN number of the book. The picture of the cover, the book title and a list of vendors will pop up showing their individual quoted buyback price of the book. The high price will also be separated in a box: On the screenshot (Raymond Chandler: Collected Stories), the box shows that TextbookRush.com is offering the highest price of $7.25 at this time. Remember, prices change all the time. You can now sell the book—click the *Sell,* and you will be taken to TextbookRush.com website to log in. It is rather simple.

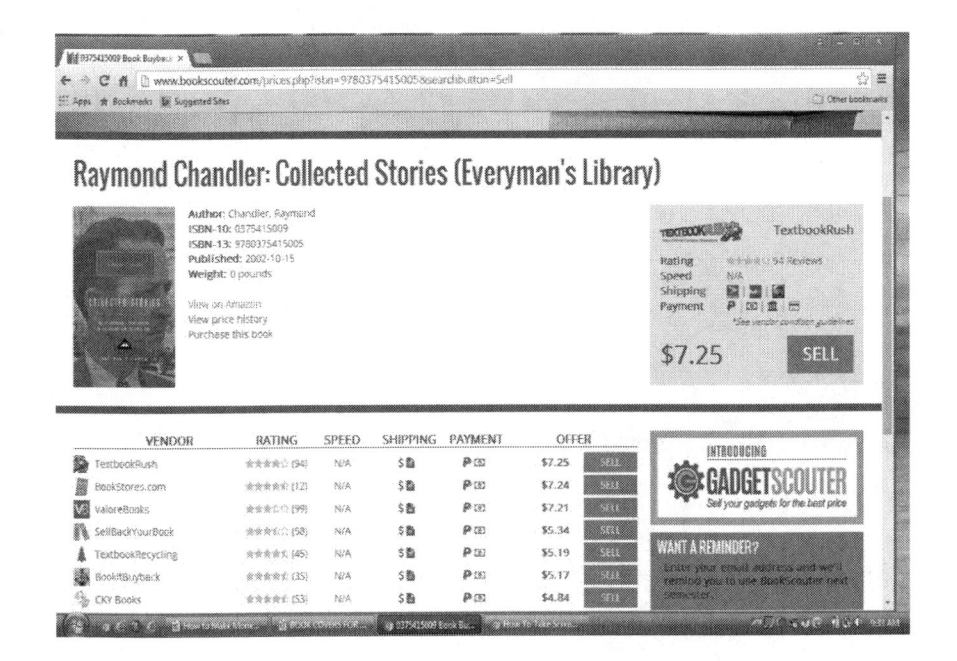

Bonavendi.com

Bonavendi gives you prices on books, DVDs, and CDs. The site has over 20 online vendors that will automatically give you a quote on your item. The site is free to use. You can also buy items for the lowest price. From their website the instructions are easily explained, but here is a short rundown:

- Enter items into the search box
- The best vendors are identified, paying the highest prices
- Sell to vendors. You now click through to the specific vendor. Bonavendi has a sidebar that has all of your items gathered for speedy processing.
- Ship items with vendor's prepaid shipping label

You will have to sign up with an account with each vendor you sell to. You will need the following:

- Email
- Password
- Name
- Address
- PayPal account (recommended for getting cash faster)
- If you do not have a PayPal account you can mark the box for a check to be sent.
- Mark the box that says you understand the buyback terms

All the buyback websites that I have encountered are similar. The information noted above is all you will need.

Smartphone Apps

Both Bookscouter and Bonavendi have smartphone Apps. If you have an IPhone or Android, you can scan a barcode of a book, DVD, CD or video game and find instantly prices dealers are willing to pay for your item. This is an extremely nice tool to have when you are at a library book sale, garage sale or swap meet. Just go to their websites and download the free Apps. Bookscouter also has a paid service and other programs for bulk sales.

This screenshot shows the same book (Collected Stories of Raymond Chandler) on Bonavenid.com. Here Amazon has the highest buyback quote of $7.78. Amazons quote is not a cash quote. It is for credit. So if you do not buy a lot of things on Amazon you are better off going with the lower cash quote from Bookstores.com or TextbookRush.com.

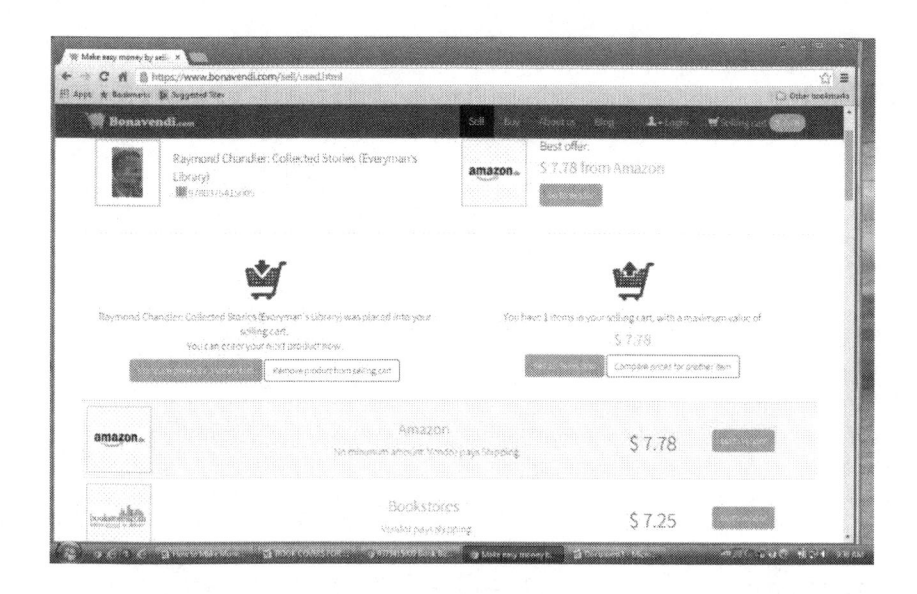

This screenshot (Coin Laundries) is another from Bookscouter.com which shows that BookitBuyBack.com (recently changed to BuyBackExpress.com) is offering the highest buyback price of $13.95. This book was purchased from a library book sale for $1.

With the same book on Bonavendi.com you can see that Amazon offers the highest quote of $16.33 (credit not cash), and Valorebooks is second with a cash offer of $11.25. So, you have an option of Amazon credit of $16.33 or BookitBuyBack.com (now BuyBackExpress.com) cash offer of $13.95. BuyBackExpress.com has just started to buyback DVDs, CDs and Video Games.

Many book buying websites are not registered with Bonavendi. Therefore, you should check with both websites when selling your books to get the best prices. Also, for DVDs and CDs you will need to go to Bonavendi since Bookscouter is only a book quote service at this time.

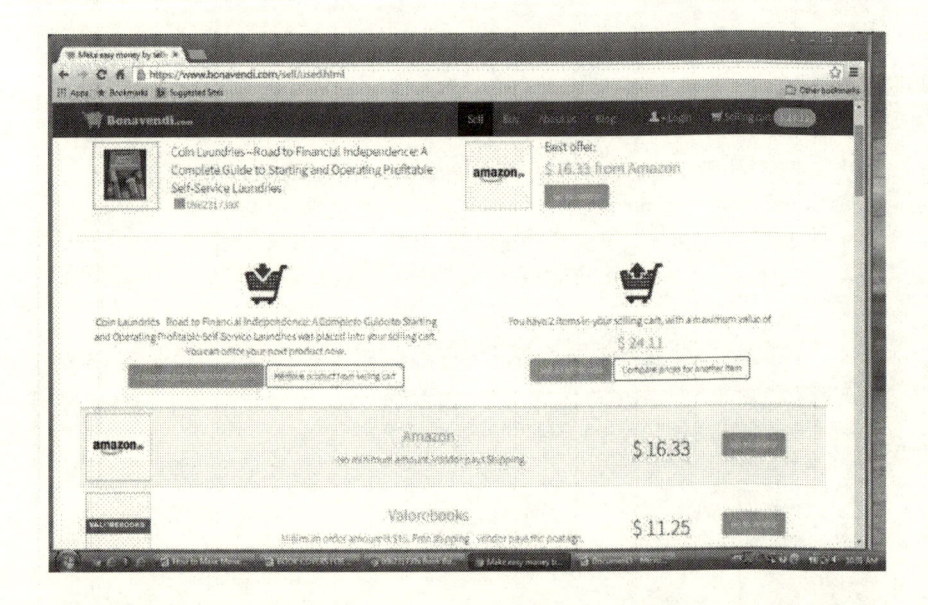

The next two screenshots show that both Bookscouter and Bonavendi have Bookbyte as offering the highest buyback at $45 for *McAlpine's Multiple Sclerosis*, 4e (4th Edition).

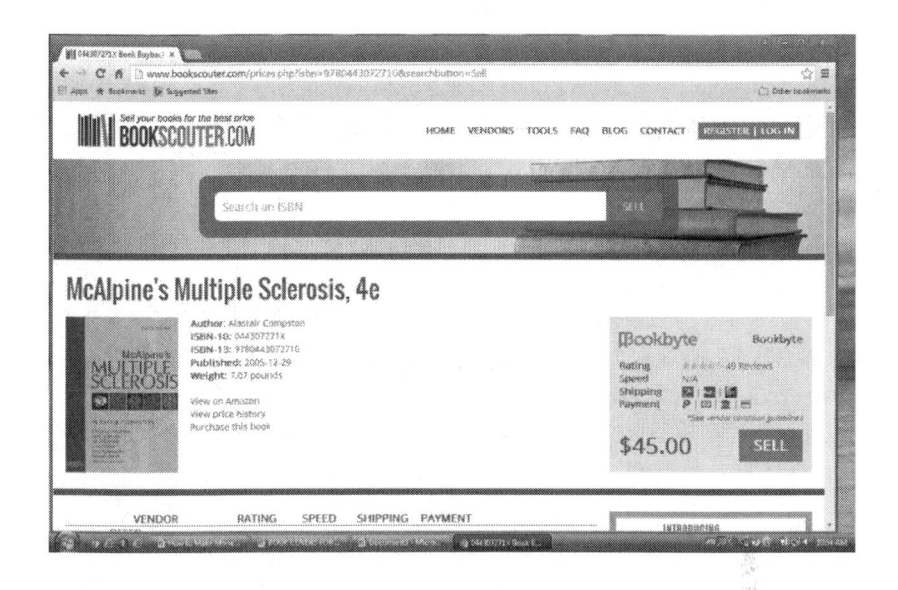

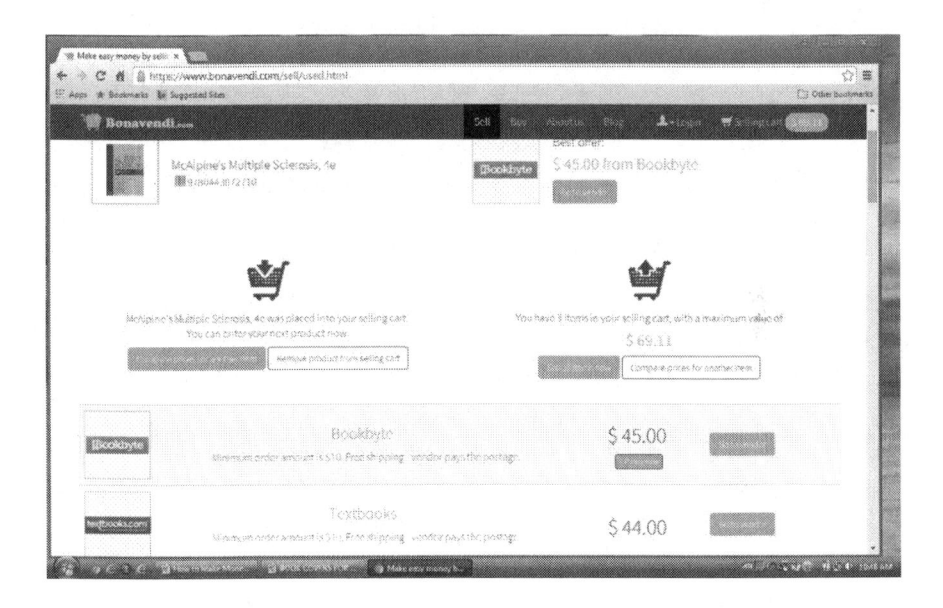

Book buyback sites other different prices and terms. Make sure to read thru their buyback terms. You also do not want to send in books with stains, missing covers, lots of writing, notations, highlighting or with heavy wear. Some sites will offer a little less for an ex-library book with stamps and stickers. Others will offer a lower price for two or more of the same books in the same order. They might quote $3 for the first copy and $2 for second. Most buyback dealers will not buy more than two of the same book on one order and many will only buy one.

Most books are not purchased by these buyback sites. And sites are changing their buyback criteria constantly. The best practice is to check out many sites and note the ones that give you the best prices. Remember, booksellers buy different types of books. One buyer might want a particular book and another may not.

Don't Ship Junk

The books you ship to dealers must be clean. Heavily marked books with lots of writing and highlighting will usually not be accepted. So, if you send in junk don't expect to be paid and don't expect the item to be returned to you.

Although, I have had a number of good experiences with SecondSpin.com, who actually returned items (DVDs, CDs) that were scratched or duplicates. In some cases the scratches were so slight I shipped the items out to another dealer, where they were accepted.

DVDs and CDs

There are four buyback companies online that I use almost exclusively for selling DVDs and CDs. My choices are primarily based on price and to a lesser extent, speed of payment. These companies buy more of what I have. First there is SellYourDVDSandCDs.com, BuyBackExpress.com, and SecondSpin.com. I fourth company I use is Amazon. Sometimes Amazon will buy items which nobody else wants. Amazon will not pay you cash, however. They will issue you credit. If you are a frequent buyer on Amazon then this works out all right, since most of what Amazon is buying from you, other dealers do not seem to want. Amazon may already have a buyer waiting for the item. I recently sold a DVD to Amazon that no other dealer quoted a buyback price. Amazon was willing to pay $12 for the item (store credit).

Most of the DVDs, CDs and video games I sell go to the following vendors:

- SellYourDVDsandCDs.com. Associated with SellBackYourBook.com

- BuyBackExpress.com. Here you can sell books, DVDs, CDs and Video Games.

- SecondSpin.com. Has a few retail stores that buy from walk-ins. Check their website for locations and times.

- Amazon.com. No cash paid, only credit for buying items on Amazon website.

Recent Transactions

The next two screenshots show recent transactions that I did with BuyBackExpress.com and Textbookrecycling.com. Most of my transactions are from $30-200 per sale. I will ship anywhere from two to five different vendors in a week.

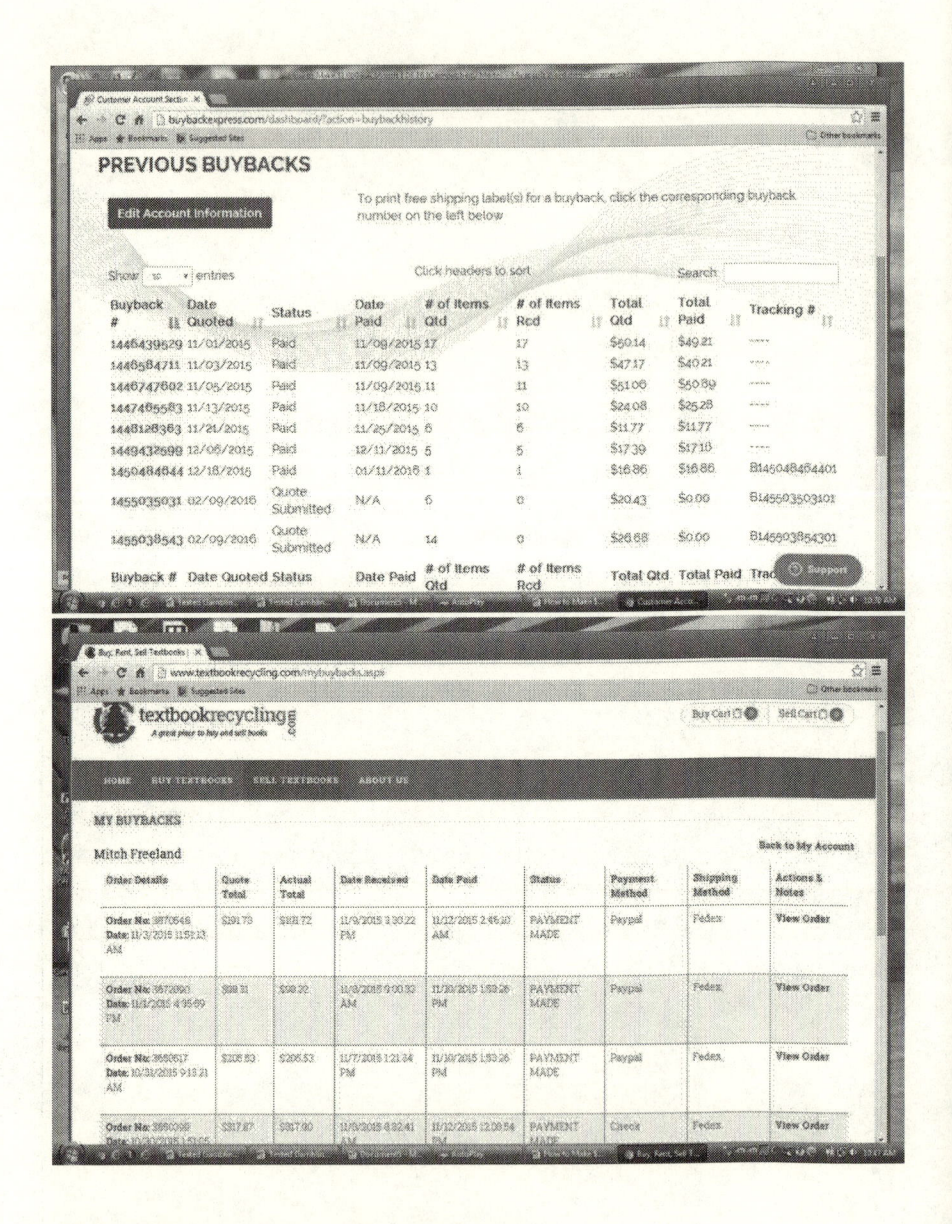

Don't Ship Incomplete Items

Is there a CD or DVD missing? If there is, and you ship the book to a dealer, it is likely you will not be paid for your book. It is also likely your book will not be shipped back to you.

With textbooks, always check for access codes, CDs and other supplemental materials.

This also goes for sets. Make sure that the book(s) that you ship are not parts of a set. A two volume set or a ten volume set in many cases have one ISBN number printed in each volume. The same number is printed in each volume and it can get confusing if you don't pay attention. Also, DVD courses such as ones from The Teaching Company, The Great Courses, come with a number of DVDs and usually a booklet. If there is no booklet, the item is incomplete. Again, these items come in many pieces but with only one ISBN number and same barcode on each piece.

Multiple Copies of the Same Item

Many dealers will not accept more than one copy of a book, DVD or CD. Contact dealers by email when you have more than one of the same item to sell. Some dealers will lower the price for your additional copies. For instance, they might quote $2 for one book, $1.75 for the second and $1 for the third copy. You have an option here: send in one copy for $2 and save the others for your next shipment, or send them all in at once and get what you can. Buyback prices fluctuate depending on supply and demand and Amazon rankings. One day a vendor is willing to pay you $7 for a book and the next day only $1.50. You will have to decide for yourself when to sell multiple copies.

Photo: Eight buyback orders ready to be packed and shipped. This is a combination of DVDs, CDs and books. Grand total of $288.43.

Boxed and ready to ship

New Items

Online buyback dealers do not distinguish your items from used to new, when, in fact, you may have many new (factory sealed) items. You may have many DVDs and CDs that are brand new and sealed, but you will only be quoted one price (a used price), for these items.

Note: SellYourDVDsandCDs.com stated that they will not accept *New*, factory sealed DVDs or CDs due to possible piracy. Therefore, if you are you might as well remove the shrink-wrap before you send it in.

There is, however, one buyback site that allows you the choice, Amazon; they offer New, Like new, or Good price quotes for DVDs and CDs. The only thing about Amazon is that it does not pay cash, only credit. If you do a lot of buying on Amazon, then it could work-out fine.

Equipment

Besides a computer, laptop and mobile phone, which you probably already have, you will also need a printer to print packing slips and mailing labels. Another handy item is a barcode scanner. Plugged directly to your computer or laptop, a scanner will let you load ISBN numbers faster by scanning barcodes.

Packing Materials and Shipping

Boxes

You will need boxes, small and large. Save all boxes, packaging paper and bubble-wrap. You will also need packing tape. If you buy a lot of things online, you will receive lots of boxes—save them! Boxes are expensive and will eat into your profits. So, save all boxes—all sizes. You will need them.

Packing Tape

Use clear tape. You do not have to use expensive tape. You can purchase inexpensive packing tape from Wal-Mart. I now use Duck Packaging Tape, 1.88 inch, 50 yd., for $1.12 a roll. When you start doing more orders, you can get the larger packs with larger rolls (100 yd.). I started out with Scotch Brand 2.5 inch form Sam's Club. It was in an eight pack for about $17.99. I use a small hand tape dispenser. You could buy one with a roll of tape on it for $2 to $3 and reuse the dispenser. For larger quantities I will search eBay for the best prices on tape. If you need just one or two rolls 99 Cent Only Stores and Harbor Freight Tools carry the same quality 2" tape for $1 each.

After you have boxed your items and secured them with packaging paper or old newspapers, or old magazine pages, tape the box securely, fold the paper prepaid mailing label and tape each size of it to the top of the box. You could use scissors to trim the table if you want to. Do not tape over the barcode. Take to post office, UPS or FEDEX, where the label suggests. That is it. You are finished. Wait about ten to twenty days and you will receive payment into your PayPal account. If you choose to receive a check it will take a week longer.

Many buyback sites are the same in that the processes involved of shipping your items and getting paid for them is similar. Allow one to two weeks for your package to arrive at the buyback facility. Packages are shipped media mail or economy ground.

Only with SecondSpin (DVDs and CDs) you pay up front for shipping. After they receive your items, they will credit you (cash added to your buyback) your postage. Sometimes, if you are sending a large package, you will not be credited for the full amount you paid. In this situation, it might be best to ship smaller orders where media mail shipping charge is not over $6 (roughly about 6 lbs.).

Chapter 5

Questions on BuyBack

"A man always has two reasons for doing anything: a good reason and the real reason."
—J. P. Morgan

Here are some general questions about buyback from vendors.

How do I get paid?
Most vendors will give you two options: You have the option of getting paid through PayPal or by check. I prefer PayPal because you'll get paid faster; and it is secure. Don't have PayPal? Visit https://www.paypal.com to sign up.

When will I get paid?
Speed seems to be everything these days so usually orders are processed as orders are received. Many companies will make a PayPal payment the same day as your order is processed, which in many cases, is the same day they receive it.

How long is the price quote good for?
Some companies will honor a quote for thirty days, and others two weeks. On many websites the vendor will post how long the quote is good for.

How do you determine your buyback prices?
Everything is set on supply and demand. The prices on books, DVDs and CDs change daily and in many cases several times a day. Many companies has specialized software that deal with pricing logistics and are based off Amazon API and are pulled several times per day, so the Buy-Back prices can be changes several times per day on active, popular books.

I heard shipping is Free – is it?
Yes, shipping is usually Free on most buyback sites!

Is my package insured?
There is some insurance with USPS, UPS and Fedex. Check with the buyback company regarding insured items. Usually, the website will have this information.

Do you receive multiple copies of a book?
All buyback websites are different. Some will buy more than one copy, but will offer a lower price for the second or three copy. Others require that you contact them.

How many books can I ship in one order?
I found this is be unlimited; but I am sure there could be a limit.

What paperwork do I need to include in my package?
Include your packing slip in each package. The packing slip has all the information on it: items shipped, price of each item, your name, and a barcode or invoicing number indentifying your package.

What is an ISBN? UPC?
An ISBN is a unique ten or thirteen digit code used to identify a book. A UPC is the unique identifier for DVDs, CDs. Each edition of a book will have its own ISBN. An ISBN can be found on the back of the book near the barcode or on the copyright page which is near the beginning of the

book. When entering an ISBN, be sure to include any leading zeros and leave out the dashes. An ISBN can end with the letter X.

Do I have to include the software that came with my book?
Yes, if it's vital to the book. DVDs, CDs, access codes essential to use of the book, or any other components that are required for usage of the book must be included. Optional components such as posters, maps, trial software, color wheels, and flash cards do not need to be included, but if available, by all means include those as well. The best way to think about what to include is to act as if you were purchasing the item you are selling - would you purchase this item with the missing components? Remember, everything you sell us is being bought by someone else - usually another student.

Do vendors purchase study guides?
Many vendors will purchase study guides, workbooks and lab manuals, but they must be free of markings and must not have missing pages. They have to be clean.

Do you buy instructor's editions or international editions?
Yes - if we are quoting a price for an item we are buyers. However, we will not purchase any item that is stamped and prohibited for resale although we may be quoting a price for a legitimate copy.

Does the condition of my books, DVDs or CDs matter?
Yes, condition matters. Your books don't have to look brand new, but they must be in good or better condition. Books can have some scratches or dings on the cover, and even some highlighting or writing. We do not purchase books with water damage, binding damage, missing pages, excessive writing or highlighting, soiled, coffee stains, sticky books, no mold, no cigarette smoke or smelly books, etc. The same goes for DVDs and CDs. Vendors will not buy scratched up DVDs or CDs. Always make sure before you send us your DVDs or CDs that the correct disc is inside. At times people forget to put the disc inside - don't be one of those people.

Do Not ship Unacceptable or Poor Condition items. Books with heavy markings (underlining, highlighting and other markings in pen or pencil), and CDs and DVDs with scratches should not be shipped. You should also replace cracked and damaged CD and DVD cases. Use rubbing alcohol to remove pen or sharpie markings on disks and cases.

What happens if I send a book, DVD or CD that isn't in good condition?
Most buyback vendors will state on their policy page that poor condition items will not be shipped back to you .

What happens if I don't include all of the items on my packing slip?
You will be paid for what was received and in most cases you will be notified by email the missing item.

What happens if I send the wrong book, DVD or CD?
If you send the incorrect item or an item that is not on your packing slip, some companies may contact you via email.

Will vendors buy books from scouts outside the United States?
Yes, but you will have to pay for your own shipping. This will most likely be an expensive shipping charge and may not make good business sense unless you are dealing with very expensive books.

Many buyback sites will pay with check but the preferred way is by Paypal. If you do not have a Paypal account you should set one up for faster payment.

PayPal® FAQ

How does PayPal work?

PayPal is used to securely send payments over the Internet. You can choose to pay from your PayPal® account balance, a credit card, debit card or bank account. To make a PayPal® purchase, select PayPal® during checkout on Go-Getter Web site and choose your method of payment. Your funds are transferred immediately and securely.

PayPal® is highly secure and committed to protecting the privacy of its users. Its industry-leading fraud prevention team is constantly developing state-of-the-art technology to keep your money and information safe. When you use PayPal® to send money, recipients never see your bank account or credit card numbers.

How Do I Contact PayPal® Customer Service?

For the fastest response, you may access the user-friendly Help Center. Developed by the PayPal® Customer Service team, this Help Center contains a comprehensive information database. Simply type a question into the search box to receive a complete answer.

If you do not find the information you need in the Help Center, PayPal® Customer Service representatives are available to assist you. Send an e-mail for a prompt response or contact PayPal® directly by phone: Customer Service: 1-402-935-2050 (a U.S. telephone number) 4:00 AM, PDT, to 10:00 PM, PDT, Monday through Friday 6:00 AM, PDT, to 8:00 PM, PDT, Saturday and Sunday. Sign up for PayPal® now.

Chapter 6

Your Step-by-Step Action Plan: A Five Step Program Getting Started

"There is no more noble occupation in the world than to assist another human being—to help someone succeed."
—Alan Loy McGinnis

This is a similar five step action plan I used in my book, *How I Make $4,000 a Month Part-Time Selling Used Books Online*. However, this plan is less complicated and much easier. Whether you are selling books or movies, the process is relatively the same. Before we begin the five step plan, you are going to have to set a budget of how much you are going to invest in product inventory. Although you really do not have *inventory* (your items are sold almost instantaneously), we'll call it inventory for now. For our example, we will use the sum of $500 starting out as you budget on inventory. This is just a number. You could start out with $20 or $50.

With $500 you can purchase roughly 500 items, a mix of Books, DVDs and CDs at $.50-$2 each. Of course, $2 is a fixed number, and you may be able to buy products cheaper. When you buy in bulk, you will pay a lower price than $2. All of my bulk purchases (200 items up) have had an average cost per item of about $1.63. Remember, price is always negotiable. The more you buy, the more the seller is apt to break down his or her price—so do not hesitate to ask.

Let us say you go out one Saturday morning and hit a few garage sales, and low and behold, one seller has hundreds of books. You start scanning and purchase your budgets worth. After you got home you took all of your books (you got 50) went to Bookscouter.com, got all the prices from the different vendors, printed your packing slips and mailing labels, packaged all the books, and dropped them off at the post office before one o'clock. You had 50 items with an average buyback of $4. You paid $1.00 per book. What is your gross profit? $150.00

Your gross sales: 50 items x $4 = $200

Minus $50 for the cost of your inventory and you are left with a $150 profit. Pretty darn simple. You simply do not have many expenses. You could deduct the price of paper, ink toner, driving mileage, and a few other incidentals; but in a nutshell that's about it. An online book scout is really an easy business.

Length of Time which you Should hold a Product

Most buyback vendors allow you two to three weeks in which the quoted buyback price is guaranteed. However, the best policy is never to hold onto inventory; sell it and ship it the same day you receive it. It will take about two weeks from the time you ship to the time you receive your money in your PayPal account.

Step 1: Getting your Equipment in Order: The Things You'll Need

Computer. A desk top or lap top—it doesn't matter as long it works well and you are comfortable with it.

Printer. A monochrome printer is your best bet for cost efficiency. I have three HP monochrome printers that are used predominantly for printed order sheets, invoices, postage labels, and thank you and introduction letters to customers. I buy generic refurbished black ink cartridges that produce about 2500 sheets before ink runs dry. Don't forget copy paper.

Hands free laser barcode scanner. A simple inexpensive scanner plugged into your computer for getting quotes will run you under $30.

Cell Phone: Download Apps for Bookscouter.com, Bonadendi.com and other buyback vendors.

Purchasing a PDA with Blue tooth laser scanner. *A PDA with a scanner and a service for getting prices on items is not necessary, but if you want to find out what items are currently selling for on Amazon and you want the extra speed, then you could look into this equipment.* You can do what I did and visit www.ASellerTool.com, check out their prices and service. Your PDA and scanner are wireless look-up devises, giving you the prices of DVDs and CDs, allowing you the opportunity to buy items knowing roughly the profits you will make by the current retail selling price of the item scanned.

A used PDA will set you back over $400 and a new Bluetooth scanner will be in $125 up range. The service of ASellerTool.com will run you $30 per month. Again, a PDA, Blue Tooth scanner, and a lookup service are not required for book scouting, but if you plan to move into selling books directly to the public, and open an Amazon Seller Account, then you will need this equipment and service.

Shipping Boxes. Save all boxes and packaging material you can. You never want to pay for boxes and packaging paper if you do not absolutely have to.

Purchase other items. Packaging tape (Scott's brand), eraser, alcohol for cleaning, Elmer's Glue, bubble-wrap and all the other materials for cleaning minor repairs and packaging. You could also use a less expensive tape such as Duck by Shur Brand. Duck is half the price of Scott's brand. You can get it at Wal-Mart for $1.12 (50 yards 2" wide roll).

After you have taken care of your basic equipment and materials needs it's now time to proceed to Step 2.

Step 2: Sign up on Bookscouter.com and Bonavendi.com

Go to Bookscouter.com and Bonavendi.com and sign-in. Although, signing up with these companies is not required, it is a good thing to do because from time-to-time you will receive special bonuses, vouchers and offers. For example: when a buyback vendor does promotions they may offer you an additional 10% to your order. Recently, SecondSpin.com offered 20% more on their buyback prices. I had shipped them $200 worth of DVDs and CDs and receive an extra $40. Because of their promotion, they paid higher prices than all of the other competing buyback vendors.

Things you will need:

- *Bank account to deposit checks or receive money from PayPal*
- *Sign up for a PayPal account*
- *Phone number and address for opening accounts with vendors*

Follow the instructions when setting up your account with vendors. You will need an email account and passwords for each vendor you sell to.

Step 3: Begin Scanning Items

When you scan or punch in the ISBN or UPC (DVDs and CDs) number (barcode number) in the Bookscouter.com or Bonavendi lookup box, the item will pop up on your screen. Check the picture, the name and the ISBN (UPC). If everything matches, then it is time to sell.

Choose the vendor with the highest buyback price. Separate items per vendor. Example: one stack will be shipped to BuyBackExpress.com another to Textbooks.com, another to Powell's and another to BookByte.com.

Once you have separated the books, DVDs and CDs, go to each of the buyback websites:

- Login to each buyback website
- Input your books (Most companies have a $10 minimum buyback, so make sure you have at least their minimum before you proceed)
- Confirm your personal information (name, address, etc.)
- Confirm method of payment (check or PayPal)
- Print Packing slip
- Print Free mailing label

Step 4: Packing and Shipping Sold Items

You can package your items on the kitchen table or on the floor for desk. Just make sure to keep the items clean and undamaged.

- Find a suitable box or poly-bubble envelope if it is only one or two items
- Use newspapers, bubble wrap or packaging paper
- Clean item with alcohol and a clean cloth
- Replace cracked and broken cases (CD and DVD cases)
- Insert sold items into box or envelop with packing slip
- Use clear 2" packing tape to secure box
- Affix mailing label with clear tape (no not place over barcodes)
- Drop off at post office, UPS or FedEx, whichever the vendor uses

Step 5: Grow Your Profits through Sourcing

Set a schedule for sourcing. If you have a full time job, a family to care for and lots of other activities that consume your time, you might only be a able to procure for a couple of hours a week. Now you will have make the time. Make a list of all sourcing venues in your area: libraries, thrift stores, swap meets and flea markets, church book sales. Check weekly on craigslist.org for garage and estate sales and private collection sales. Check with Booksalefinder.com. Plan your sourcing weeks in advance and stick to your schedule.

CONGRATULATIONS! YOU'VE FINISHED

I hope you found the information in this book helpful. Becoming a book scout has never been easier. You can now get a quote from an online vendor prior to buying anything—and you can get it right from your phone. You do not have to spend a lot of time to make money as a book scout. All you have to do is be prepared. Download your book scout Apps from Bookscouter.com and Bonavendi.com and you are ready to go.

Thank you, again.

M. Mitch Freeland

HAPPY SCOUTING

APPENDIX 1

Frequently Asked Questions For Book Scouting at Library Book Sales

How many books can I expect to acquire from a quarterly or semiannual Library sale?

Good quarterly and semiannual sales with five thousand to ten thousand books available can produce thirty to eighty or more worthwhile books, given the usual competition.

What should be expected from large or mega Library sales held once or twice per year?

Sales that advertise 25,000 books up are sometimes the most populated when it comes to aggressive buyers. These sales also run for several days. The first day you should expect twenty-five to fifty books or more and around the same for the second day if new books are brought out or the books have gone half price. Because books at large events are typically priced individually, you'll unfortunately come into contact with some valuable books you will not buy since they will not be economically suitable. However, by the second day of the sale, some of these books will now make sense since they are half the price from the previous day; for example, a book with a resale value of $30 with an Amazon ranking of 250,000 will not be a suitable investment when the asking price is $30. Remember, you do not want to eat up a lot of cash. However, when the price is slashed in half to $4 it now will make economic sense and your capital risk is minimized. Your selling price can drop $15 and you'll still be in fair shape for a decent profit.

What if there aren't many sales in my area?
You'll have to travel out of your area if you want to attain more sales. Typically, I will travel over a hundred miles each way to sales. The average monthly sales I attend are well over thirty miles each way.

Should I join the Friends of the Library?
Yes. Not only are you able to buy books at the preview sale, but now you are also on their mailing list and e-mail list. Many libraries do not advertise their book sales on booksalefinder.com or other internet sites—because of this, resellers and dealers, especially new players in the game are often not informed of pending sales. Some of these sales are very good since few resellers are aware of them. Annual memberships range for $5-$40. Most annual memberships are from $10-$15.

Should I volunteer?
I suggest volunteering to help sort books prior to every sale. But you do not want to spend hours doing this. Sometimes you'll be able to purchase books before the sale. You'll also get a sneak peek of all the books available allowing you an opportunity to know where to go when the doors open. Volunteering for fifteen minutes before a sale can be well worth your time. It's a great feeling knowing exactly where the prime books are before the sale begins. Volunteering can be worth hundreds if not thousands of dollars to you over the course of a year. When I'm talking about volunteering I'm not talking several hours—I'm referring to just a few minutes prior to the sale, ten to thirty minutes

Should I attend sales that advertise that they sell online?
Yes. Some sales will only sell a few books online and others a lot—but you'll never know until you attend. Also, when a library announces that

more expensive books are sold online, it may also be advertising to dealers not to attend. Valuable books do slip through the cracks.

Can I get in early if I'm disabled?
If you are disabled always call the friends of the Library prior to sales day and ask if they allow disabled persons to shop for books before the preview sale or general sale should there not be a preview sale. Clearly explain your situation. There is a good change you may get in early and score. Whether you use a walker, wheelchair, or cane, explain your situation clearly. Many volunteers are in their second half of living and will understand your situation.

What should I focus on first at the sale?
Your number one mission is to acquire valuable books. Many of the more valuable books will be textbooks and other nonfiction books. You should focus on speed and concentration—moving stealthily in a crowded room can be a skill to be learned.

Do I really need a scanner or smart phone at book sales?
Yes. There are so many books at an average sale that are not worth even ten cents online. Therefore, a scanner or smart phone becomes an absolute necessity if you are serious about selling books and making money.

Other than books could I focus or specialize in DVDs?
Yes, but usually there are more books and fewer DVDs or CDs available and library book sales. Most libraries sell DVDs for higher prices than the average book—especially set's as T.V. series. The DVD market, movies in particular, are also much more competitive. Prices on DVDs fluctuate faster on the way down because the supply is greater. There are also some very large players in the DVD market—players who are extremely competitive on pricing and for you to compete with them on the way down is fool hearty. Other than movies, instructional courses on

DVD with smaller volume cuts do better and prices hold for the most part. Older movies on DVD do better than current movies. Courses, "how-to's", exercise and training programs hold value better than most current movies. Look particularly for older T. V. series, documentaries, PBS and specialized exercise DVDs.

How do I find out about libraries that do not advertise their sales aggressively?
Do a quick search online for libraries in your city or county. Get their phone numbers and call them up and ask if they have book sales or a bookstore. For instance, if I lived in Fresno, California, I'd go to Google and search *Libraries Fresno* or *Libraries Fresno Book Sale*.

Do the volunteer friends of the library get all the good books before the sale?
No. Unless there are some resellers in the bunch, but my experience indicates that the volunteers only pick out a few books that they are interested in—and most of these are typically current popular novels not nonfiction or textbooks.

How early should I get to a sale?
This depends on the size of the sale and how aggressively it was promoted. You can show up at most regular monthly and quarterly sales about an hour before the event. If the sale is a large sale try two hours and it the sale is a mega sale try the night before. It is always smart to call the friends before you go to a sale you've not attended before and ask: When does a line start forming? A volunteer who's been around a while should give you a reliable answer.

How aggressively should I try to negotiate with volunteers to get a deal on books that I think are priced too high at a Library book sale?

The best time to negotiate is late in the sale, when many buyers, and most resellers and dealers have already purchased their items and left. Don't forget, that the "Friends" want to sell everything that they've haul out to sell.

Pick the few books out that you want to negotiate for a lower price—the more you have the better deal you'll get. If you have five books and they are all priced differently and the total combined price for all is $60, you should ask "What's the best price I can get for all these together?" You're hoping for an answer of "How about $10. And the negotiation is over—you'll pay $10. This will happen in about a third of the time. It's that easy. All you have to do is ask.

Other times the individual authorized to give discounts on items will cut the price in half and that now will become your starting point to negotiate. Here's an example from a recent sale:

The sale had been going for about two hours. Nearly all the dealers had done. I wanted four book bible set which was worth $250. They had priced each book for $20. I wasn't willing to pay $80. After I asked 'what's the best you could do for this set,' she dropped the price to $10 each, $40 for the set. I told her I was hoping for about $5 each, $20 for the set. She said, 'how about $30.' I agreed and paid the $30.

You can't negotiate early in the sale. So get the good stuff in your box first. Disregard its price. You want to get it off the market so you'll have a chance to negotiate a lower price later in the sale.

Plan to negotiate for lower prices on higher priced items at every sale. Most people don't—and never will. This gives you a huge edge to get a big haul when a lot of the more expensive items are not sold and the sun is setting.

Plan to negotiate aggressively, but tactfully. Do not be rude, or offensive, and do not behave like a whining cheapskate. Be courteous, pleasant and respectful. And do not beg—you'll be coming back to this sale again.

Is it unethical to hoard books at a sale?
No. If hoarding in prohibited at any particular sale you would naturally not hoard. Some may feel guilty about it, thinking they are behaving unethically, but it has nothing to do with ethics. If you do not get books off the tables and into your box, others will. The activity is fast at the start of a sale and you'll have to do what you can to protect your interest.

How much is too much to pay for an item at a sale?
It depends on what the buyback is. If a book costs $1 and an online vendor is offering to buy it for $2, then buy it. If you bought twenty books for $1 and sold them for $2, you made 100% on your money. But usually, you will do a lot better than this. You can lock in your sell price even before you invest a penny buying any item. As long as your phone in working and you have an internet connection and, you are in business.

What if I only want to sell DVDs and CDs should I still go to library sales?
Yes. Attend as many sales as possible. Once you've gone to enough sales, you should be able to determine which sales are worth your while and which are not. Most libraries do not get very many donated DVDs or CDs—books remain the number one item. Make it a habit to hoard as many DVDs once the sale begins, especially when the pickings are slim. Should you decide to specialize in non-book items plan to be first in line at the sale and rush straight to the DVD and CD section and drop (hoard) as many DVDs in your box first, scan the CDs. Lastly, scan the DVDs in your box and return the ones that have little value.

Do you think in the future all libraries will begin selling their more valuable books online?
I do not think all libraries will sell their more expensive books online, but many will. I do think that the opportunity to find value online is quite easy, and feel most libraries will look-up books online and price books at sales according to their perceived value or at a price considerably more

than $1 or $2. For example, a book selling online for $50 might be priced for $10-$15 at a sale; not the typical $1 or $2 price.

Would You Like to Know More?

You can learn a lot more about book scouting and making a living selling used books online in my other eBooks or paperbacks.

What else?

I frequently run special promotions where I offer free or discounted books (usually $ 0.99 eBooks) on **MitchFreeland.com** and **MitchWrites.com (coming soon)**. One way to get instant notifications for these deals is to subscribe to my email list. By joining, you receive updates on the latest offer, you'll also get a free copy of my "*Mini Goals Huge Results*" book.

Visit me at www.MitchFreeland.com

Did You Like *How to Make $1,000+*?

Before you go, I'd like to say "thank you" for buying my book. I know you could have picked from dozens of books online bookselling, but you took a chance with me. So a big thanks for getting this book or buying the paperback and reading all the way to the end. Now I would like to ask for a *small* favor.

If you liked this book and found it helpful, could you please take a minute and leave a positive review on the website you bought this book from. Your feedback will help me continue to write the kind of books that help you get results. And if you liked it and found it helpful, then please let me know.

Thank you, again.

M. Mitch Freeland

WHAT'S NEXT?

Author of Mastering the Art of Sourcing for Online Booksellers & Collectors and How to Identify First Editions

M. MITCH FREELAND

HOW I MAKE $4,000 A MONTH PART-TIME SELLING USED BOOKS ONLINE

The Authoritative Manual

How Ordinary People Like Me are Making $50,000+ Selling Used Books Part-time from Home & How You Can Too!

"...I have followed Mr. Freeland's plan, and can honestly say to my delight that it works! If you're looking for an alternative and interesting way to make some additional money, I wholeheartedly recommend you purchase this e-book."—MK457

DISCOVER: How to Create a Successful Online Bookstore from Home Starting from Scratch!

How I Make $4,000 a Month Part-time Selling Used Books Online is the most up-to-date book on online bookselling available Today! Jam packed with everything you need and more to get you started. Mitch Freeland gives it to you straight with solid information you can rely on.

You will Learn How Ordinary People just like you are making $50,000+ Selling Used Books Online, and from Home.

Starting from scratch and starting from home, you earn what you want in no time. Yes, you can run a thriving business straight from your home.

Mitch Freeland guides you every step of the way toward building a solid business that allows you to have the freedom, joy and fulfillment of creating something meaningful for you and your family.

Brand new entrepreneurs wanting to build a new, successful online business that generates income 24/7 from home can benefit from the strategies revealed in this book. Everyone who dreams of a lifestyle change and freedom from the burdens of working for someone else now has the answers to their most pressing questions regarding an online bookselling business.

Books, DVDs, CDs and VHS tapes are the perfect products to sell. You don't need to manufacture anything, and unlike other businesses, selling books online means...

- No spending thousands on a monthly lease for retail space or office
- No daily commutes to a job that leaves you unfulfilled
- No expensive equipment to buy
- No unreliable wholesalers or vendors to deal with

In *How I Make $4,000 a Month Part-time Selling Used Books Online,* **you will learn it all:**

- How to set up your online business from home
- The habits of successful online booksellers
- How to get quality inventory to sell
- How to list inventory correctly and how to pack and ship items when sold
- Where to go for supplies and which equipment to use
- How to deal with customers and receive high positive feedback
- All the custom forms and letters that Freeland created for superior customer relations
- You will learn how to grow your business into a going concern for the long-term

Do you have a dream of working your own business from home? It's a good dream; but it doesn't have to be just a dream. I've done it and you can too.

You can start right NOW where you are!

Order your Copies Today at

| www.MitchFreeland.com |

Or ask your local bookstore or librarian to order it

How I Make $4,000 a Month Part-Time Selling Used Books Online

Buy at your Favorite Online Bookstore

How about......

M. MITCH FREELAND

Author of *How I Make $4,000 a Month Part-Time Selling Used Books Online* & *Caring for Books*

MASTERING THE ART OF SOURCING FOR ONLINE BOOKSELLERS & COLLECTORS

The Most Comprehensive Study on Book and Media Sourcing Available!

How to Buy Books, DVDs, CDs and VHS tapes for at least 80% below Market Value

**Have you ever marveled at successful booksellers and book collectors and wondered where they find their valuable books, DVDs, CDs?
Well, in this book you are going to find out.**

What is sourcing? In short, sourcing is where you get the products you sell. To start a business, run a business and grow a business you need to be an expert at sourcing. You need to find the best products at a low acquisition cost, resulting in high profit margins. In *Mastering the Art of Sourcing*…you are going to get the most comprehensive work on sourcing for booksellers and collectors available.

Sourcing is a art. It is also a skill that is learnable and can be mastered. You are going to master the art using this book, your step-by-step guide.

In *Mastering the Art of Sourcing*…I'll *show* you how to:
- source better
- save time and money with efficient scheduling
- get more products
- negotiate like a professional on large purchases
- source multiple venues in a day
- evaluate product salability—what to buy and not buy
- deal with private sellers and Friends of the Library organizations
- built relationships and long-term alliances with important sources
- follow strategies that will knock the socks off your competitors
- have all the necessary tools at your disposal to propel your enterprise from a home operation with rapid growth to a multi-faceted venture with the potential expansion into multi-media products and beyond.
-

Why Wait? Available Now at
www.MitchFreeland.com

Mastering the Art of Sourcing for Online Booksellers & Collectors
At Fine Stores Everywhere

GET YOUR FREE BOOK
www.MitchFreeland.com

Did you know less than 10 percent of the population has goals? Even fewer, 3 percent, have written, specific and measurable goals.

Studies show people with goals succeed faster and with better results than people without goals. Did you know that nearly all high achievers set goals in some form or fashion? From athletes, business people, entrepreneurs, educators and world leaders, all have goals: big ones, small ones and *mini-goals*.

A goal is not a wish or lucky manifestation. A goal is something you pursue to make you and yours better, safer or richer.

A goal achieved is a product of daily diligence and consistent effort. A *worthy* goal is a goal that benefits you and everyone associated with you: family, friends, employees, co-workers, and customers. A good goal, a worthy goal, benefits many people whether realized or not.

In *Mini Goals Huge Results*, you will discover how to:

- Set mini goals related to family, career, health and fitness, financial, religious and spirituality goals, and personal and physical wants goals.
- Create mini goals that lead to the achievement of large goals
- Visualize the process toward successful goal achievement
- Create specific affirmations that are tested to produce results
- Motivate yourself and articulate your vision and why having goals, written down, work toward life-long happiness
- Set Mini-Goals to combat non-clinical depression
- Create positive, long-lasting change
- Transform your life with Mini Goals using an easy 7 Step Process

Identify your Mini Goals, achieve success, and defeat the fear of failure!

More Books
by M. MITCH FREELAND

Writer, publisher, investor, poker player, gambler, real estate investor, and businessman, M. Mitch Freeland has been called the *modern day polymath*. A prolific writer, he has authored over sixty books and continues to write daily on his interests.

Online Bookselling

How I Make $4,000 a Month Part-Time Selling Used Books Online

How to Make $1,000+ Online as a Part-Time Book Scout

Mastering the Art of Sourcing for Online Booksellers and Collectors

How to Identify First Editions (Spring 2019)

Caring for Books: A Repair and Preservation Handbook for Booksellers, Collectors, Book Lovers and Librarians Interested in Improving the Condition of their Books

Casino Gaming Books

Winning Craps: How to Play and Win Like a Pro. Learn How I Beat the Craps Out of the Casinos for 30 Years

Tested Gambling Systems That Can Make You $100,000+ a Year: Craps, Horses, Poker, Blackjack

How to Play Craps and Win: The 3 Irrefutable Winning Plays and How to Profit from Them

How to Win at Casino Craps

How to Play Baccarat

How to Count Cards at Blackjack

How to Play Blackjack for Beginners and Win! Learn Basic and Advanced Strategies for Optimum Winning Play

Horse Racing: The Systems

Poker Books

The Small Stakes Poker Hustle: How I Make $3,500+ A Month Part-Time Playing $1-$2 & $1-$3 No-Limit Hold'em & How You Can Too!

Poker Tells and Body Language: How to Substantially Improve Your Income by Studying Your Opponents Mannerisms and Eccentricities

Cash Poker: How to Make $250,000 Over the Next 5 Years Playing Small Stakes Poker

The Poker System: How to Play No-Limit Texas Hold'em: A Primer for Smart New Players Who Want to Start with A Winning Edge in the World's Greatest Poker Game

Tactical Player Isolation at No-Limit Hold'em

How to Become an A+ Student at Poker

Real Estate Books by
M. MITCH FREELAND and JOHN FREELAND

The Millionaire Real Estate Flippers

The Millionaire Real Estate Landlords

How to Make Real Estate More Valuable

How to Rent Your House, Duplex, Triplex & Other Multi-Family Property Fast!

The Real Estate Hustle

5 Day Flip: How to Get Offers Accepted Fast on Fixer-Uppers

For information on any of these titles visit us at:
www.MitchFreeland.com

SPECIAL SALES

Books published by Las Vegas Book Company are available at special quantity discounts worldwide to be used for training or for use in corporate promotional programs. Quantity discounts are available to corporations, educational institutions and charitable organizations. Personalized front or back covers and endpapers can be produced in large numbers. If you are interested in exploring options for bulk purchase, of ten or more copies, send us an email for discounts.

We encourage you to share this book with others:

- Give this book to friends as a gift
- Give a book to your children or students
- Present this book on your website or blog
- Link your site to www.MitchFreeland.com
- Write a book review for your local paper, your favorite magazine, school, or a website you spend time on. Place your review on Amazon or Goodreads.
- Introduce us on radio stations or pod casts—author guest
- Display this book at your shop or business on the counter for resale to customers. Email us at MMitchFreeland@gmail.com for wholesale rates on bulk orders and volume discounts
- Review a copy for your newsletters, schools papers and magazines, websites, and review journals
- Buy a set of books for the Boys and Girls Clubs in your community, Churches, and fundraising organizations.
- Mention this book on your email lists
- Share this book with family members, friends, and co-workers who may need a motivational or financial boost

Let us know how we can best serve you.
 For information, contact us at:
www.MitchFreeland.com or MMitchFreeland@gmail.com

BOOK SCOUTING LOG

PLACE	DATE	#BOOKS	$INVESTED	$SOLD

BOOK SCOUTING LOG

PLACE	DATE	#BOOKS	$INVESTED	$SOLD

BOOK SCOUTING LOG

PLACE	DATE	#BOOKS	$INVESTED	$SOLD

PREFERRED BUYBACK WEBSITES

NAME	ADDRESS	WEBSITE	PHONE

PREFERRED SCOUTING VENUE

PLACE: _____ PHONE: _____

ADDRESS: _____ WEBSITE: _____

CONTACT PERSON: _____

DAYS AND HOURS OF OPERATION: _____

PLACE: _____ PHONE: _____

ADDRESS: _____ WEBSITE: _____

CONTACT PERSON: _____

DAYS AND HOURS OF OPERATION: _____

PLACE: _____ PHONE: _____

ADDRESS: _____ WEBSITE: _____

CONTACT PERSON: _____

DAYS AND HOURS OF OPERATION: _____

PLACE: _____ PHONE: _____

ADDRESS: _____ WEBSITE: _____

CONTACT PERSON: _____

DAYS AND HOURS OF OPERATION: _____

PREFERRED SCOUTING VENUE

PLACE: _____ PHONE: _____

ADDRESS: _____ WEBSITE: _____

CONTACT PERSON: _____

DAYS AND HOURS OF OPERATION: _____

PLACE: _____ PHONE: _____

ADDRESS: _____ WEBSITE: _____

CONTACT PERSON: _____

DAYS AND HOURS OF OPERATION: _____

PLACE: _____ PHONE: _____

ADDRESS: _____ WEBSITE: _____

CONTACT PERSON: _____

DAYS AND HOURS OF OPERATION: _____

PLACE: _____ PHONE: _____

ADDRESS: _____ WEBSITE: _____

CONTACT PERSON: _____

DAYS AND HOURS OF OPERATION: _____

Made in the USA
San Bernardino, CA
08 May 2019